COACHING FOR PERFORMANCE

A Practical Guide to Growing Your Own Skills

John Whitmore

Pfeiffer
& COMPANY

Amsterdam • Johannesburg • Oxford
San Diego • Sydney • Toronto

PUBLISHED BY ARRANGEMENT WITH NICHOLAS BREALEY PUBLISHING LTD,
14 STEPHENSON WAY, LONDON NW1 2HD, UK. FOR SALE IN NORTH AMERICA
ONLY AND NOT FOR EXPORT THEREFROM.

Published in the United States by
Pfeiffer & Company
8517 Production Avenue
San Diego, CA 92121-2280

Page Compositor: Terry Journey

ISBN: 0-89384-238-9

Printed in the United States of America.
Printing 1 2 3 4 5 6 7 8 9 10

Contents

Acknowledgments

*A*ny book of this nature will be the product of the author's exposure to and learning from many experiences and many people.

Tim Gallwey, as the creator of the Inner Game, must undoubtedly head the list, followed in chronological order by Bob Kriegel, Sarah Ferguson, Graham Alexander, Alan Fine, Caroline Harris, Chris Morgan, Ben Cannon, Miles Downey, and Peter Lightfoot, who all started as Inner Game sports coaches and who have since applied their coaching skills in business with great effect. I would recommend each of them as excellent coaches, along with Drs. Alan Beggs and Lew Hardy, who also provided academic respectability to Inner Game ideas, which encouraged us when rejection by traditionalists was widely available.

I am especially grateful to my two most recent coaching colleagues, David Hemery and David Whitaker, with whom I have taught countless courses and shared creative ideas. Both were successful performers and coaches who reached Olympian heights, and similar conclusions to the rest of us, through their own experiences. I am grateful also to the National Coaching Foundation, Richard Evans and especially to David Evans, chief executive of the Grass Roots Group PLC, which provided the forums through which the three of us were able to pursue our coaching ambitions. It was in Grass Roots time that I wrote this book.

My closest family has made a very big contribution. My wife Diana, who runs an educational charity that trains psychotherapists and counselors, has monitored the development of my people skills over the years, keeping me in line with conventional wisdom and guiding me through the minefield of the deeper aspects of the human psyche. My son Jason is still only nine but is already an outstanding skier and tennis player. Almost daily he reaffirms my faith in people's potential to learn fast and perform at a very high level without the need to resort to the usual expected, and in my opinion excessive, amount of external technical input.

Finally, thanks to Tim Davison, Nick Brealey, and Marion Russell, who have given me feedback, encouragement, criticism, and suggestions that have made this a far better book than it might otherwise have been.

Introduction

*C*oaching is the current buzzword in business circles. Attend any gathering of executives, personnel directors, human resource experts, entrepreneurs, or trainers and you cannot fail to hear the word "coaching" spoken as frequently as "profit" or "recession." Unfortunately, the popularizing of this new term has led both the well-meaning and the unscrupulous to apply it to their old wares. Consequently coaching is in danger of being misrepresented, misperceived, and dismissed as not so new and different, and for failing to live up to its promises. Furthermore, many high-level executives genuinely believe that they are democratic and that they use coaching as a matter of course. Since such people receive no feedback to the contrary, and their subordinates would never dare to enlighten them, in ignorance they continue to demean both their work force and the value of coaching.

More Than a Buzzword

The purpose of this book is to put the record straight by describing and illustrating what coaching really is, what it can be used for, when and how much it can be used, who can use it well, and who cannot. Contrary to the attractive claims of Ken Blanchard's *The One-Minute Manager*, there are no quick fixes in business, and good coaching is a skill, an art perhaps, that requires a depth of understanding and plenty of practice if it is to deliver its astonishing potential. Reading this book will not turn you into an expert coach, but it will help you to recognize the enormous value and potential of coaching, and perhaps set you on a journey of self-discovery that will have a profound effect on your business success, your

The Skill, Art, and Practice of Coaching

1

sporting and other skills, and how you relate to others at work and at home.

Gender

Throughout this book I will more often use the masculine gender, not because I am sexist, which I am not, nor because I abhor the literary clumsiness of "he or she" and "his or her," which I do, but because it is men who need to heed its message most. In the coaching courses my colleagues and I run, women have consistently shown more natural ability in adopting a coaching philosophy. It is more in line with their style. Perhaps the influx of more and more women into senior management roles will help to establish coaching as the communication norm throughout business. I hope so, and I hope that some of them will find the coaching model in this book useful.

Hire a Coach or Grow Your Own?

The business leader is faced with a choice between hiring a skilled consultant coach on a regular basis for specific functions such as boardroom facilitation, troubleshooting, team development or skill acquisition, or training himself and his colleagues in coaching. The choice is not an easy one and will depend on many factors, and while one or the other may be preferable for particular circumstances, the ideal would be to use both.

I hope this book will help the chief executives, human resource directors, and others who read it to clarify their needs and to make their best decisions. All people who truly understand coaching will soon begin to coach themselves on everything from career choices to their golf swings to those very personal issues that they would be most reluctant to share with another. After all, self-coaching is a safe way to practice and develop the skill of coaching, which can then be applied to others with confidence.

Self-Coaching

I will use examples and analogies from business and from a variety of sports to illustrate particular points, and, to clarify the process further, I will provide the dialogue of an imaginary but typical coaching session. There is also a table of standard questions, which could form the basis of a coaching session, questions upon which the coach would build and elaborate according to the particular circumstances.

What Is Coaching? 1

T^{*he*} dictionary defines the verb *to coach* as to "tutor, train, give hints to, prime with facts." This does not help us much, for those things can be done in many ways, some of which bear no relationship to coaching. Coaching is as much about the way these things are done as about what is done. Coaching is primarily concerned with the type of relationship between the coach and the coachee, and the means and style of communication used. The "facts" are secondary, and you will see why later. Of course, the objective of improving performance is paramount, but how that is best achieved is what is in question.

THE SPORTS ORIGINS OF COACHING

For some reason we have tennis *coaches* but ski *instructors*. Both, for the most part, are instructors. In recent years tennis instruction has become somewhat less dogmatic and technique-based, but it still has a very long way to go.

The Inner Game

The teaching of skiing and tennis, as well as golf, was tackled more than a decade ago by Harvard educator and tennis expert Timothy Gallwey. He threw down the gauntlet with a book titled *The Inner Game of Tennis*, quickly followed by *Inner Skiing*, and *The Inner Game of Golf*. The word *inner* was used to indicate the player's internal state or, to use Gallwey's words, "the opponent within one's own head is more formidable than the one the other side of the net." Anyone who has had one of those days on the court when he couldn't do anything right will recognize what Gallwey is referring to. Gallwey went on to claim that if a coach can help a player to remove or reduce the internal obstacles to his performance, an unexpected natural ability will flow forth without the need for much technical input from the coach.

At the time Gallwey's books first appeared, few coaches, instructors, or pros could believe, let alone embrace, his ideas, although players devoured them eagerly in bestseller-list quantities. The professionals' entire approach to their work was threatened. They thought Gallwey was trying to turn the teaching of sports on its head and that he was undermining their egos, their authority, and their principles. In a way he was, but their fears exaggerated their fantasies about his intentions. He was not threatening them with unemployment, but merely proposing that they would be more effective if they changed their approach.

The Essence of Coaching

And Gallwey *had* put his finger on what is the essence of coaching. *Coaching is unlocking a person's potential to maximize their own performance. It is helping them to learn rather than teaching them.*

This was not new: Socrates had voiced the same things some two thousand years earlier, but somehow his philosophy had been lost in the rush to materialism of the last two centuries. The pendulum has swung back and coaching, if not Socrates, is back and here to stay for a generation or two! Gallwey's books coincided with the emergence in psychological understanding of a more optimistic model of humankind than the old behaviorist view that we are little more than empty vessels into which everything has to be poured. The new model suggested we are more like an acorn, which contains within it all the potential to be a magnificent oak tree. We need nourishment and encouragement, but the "oak-tree" is already within us.

If we accept this model, then the way we learn, and, more importantly, the way we teach and instruct, must be questioned. Unfortunately, habits die hard and methods persist, even though their limitations are obvious. Universal proof of success of new methods has been hard to demonstrate because few have understood and used them fully, and many others have been unwilling to set aside old proven ways for long enough to reap the rewards of new ones. Recently, however, as much through necessity as progress, worker participation, delegation of responsibility, accountability, and coaching have found their way into business language.

FROM SPORTS TO BUSINESS

Even if some managers were philosophically sympathetic to the Socratic method, coaching remained academic. Tim Gallwey was perhaps the first to demonstrate a simple but comprehensive method of coaching that could be readily applied to almost any situation. It is hardly surprising that Gallwey found himself lecturing more often to business leaders than to sportspeople. His books did not attempt to teach coaching, but rather identified the issues we so often face in sports and business and gave clues as to how to overcome them ourselves. The coaching method was too vulnerable to distortion by the prevailing attitudes and beliefs of the would-be coach for it to be taught through a book alone, and this is a problem that I face now.

I did, however, seek out Tim Gallwey, was trained by him, and founded the Inner Game in Britain. We soon formed a small team of Inner Game coaches. At first all coaches were trained by Gallwey, but later we trained our own. We ran Inner Tennis courses and Inner Skiing holidays, and many golfers freed up their swings with Inner Golf. It was not long before our sporting clients began to ask us if we could apply the same methods to prevailing issues in their companies. We did, and all the leading proponents of business coaching today graduated from or were profoundly influenced by the Gallwey school of coaching.

Inner Business

Through years of experience in the business field, we have built and elaborated on those first methods and adapted them to the issues and conditions of today's business environment. Some of us have specialized in teaching managers to coach; others have acted as independent coaches for executives and for business teams. Although we are competitors with one another in the field, we remain close friends and frequently work together. This in itself speaks highly of the method, for it was Tim Gallwey who suggested that your opponent in tennis is really your friend if he makes you stretch and run. He is not a friend if he just pats the ball back to you, as that will not help you to improve your game, and isn't that what we are all trying to do in our different fields?

Mentoring

Finally, because I am defining coaching, I should perhaps mention *mentoring*, another word that has recently crept into business parlance. The word originates from Greek mythology, in which Odysseus, when setting out for Troy, entrusted his house and the education of Telemachus to his friend, mentor. "Tell him all you know," Odysseus said, and thus he unwittingly set some limits to mentoring. A modern-day mentor was Mike Sprecklen, the coach to the winning rowers, Holmes and Redgrave. "I was stuck, I had taught them all I knew technically," Sprecklen said on his completion of a performance coaching course, "but this opens up the possibility of going further, for they can feel things that I can't even see." He had discovered a new way forward with them, working from their experiences and perceptions rather than from his own. Good coaching and good mentoring can and should take a performer beyond the limitations of the coach or mentor's own knowledge.

In practice and in business, mentoring has come to be used interchangeably with coaching, as stated in David Clutterbuck's book, *Everyone Needs a Mentor:*

> In spite of the variety of definitions of mentoring (and the variety of names it is given, from coaching or counseling to sponsorship) all the experts and communicators appear to agree that it has its origins in the concept of apprenticeship, when an older, more experienced individual passed down his knowledge of how the task was done and how to operate in the commercial world.

Eric Parsloe, in his book *Coaching, Mentoring and Assessing*, does make a slight distinction by suggesting that coaching is

> directly concerned with the immediate improvement of performance and development of skills by a form of tutoring or instruction. Mentoring is always one step removed and is concerned with the longer-term acquisition of skills in a developing career by a form of advising and counseling.

I advocate an advising or counseling format as stated in Parsloe's explanation of mentoring, as opposed to instruction. I apply mentoring, however, with equal validity and effect to immediate performance improvement and to skill development, both short- and long-term. It can be "hands on" and it can be "one step removed"; either way, I call it coaching. Whether we label it coaching, advising, counseling, or mentoring, if done well, the underlying principles and methodology remain the same. If the principles on which this book elaborates are neglected, staff and performance will suffer, and no nice, new names will help them!

The Manager As Coach 2

*H*ere lies the paradox: The manager traditionally holds the paycheck, the key to promotion, and also the ax. This is fine so long as you believe the only way to motivate is through the judicious application of the carrot and the stick. But it is my view that if you treat people like donkeys, they will behave like donkeys. Donkeys will do as little as they can get away with.

The Carrot and the Stick

That money motivates is not in question, but if it comes in the form of minimal increases, toughly negotiated and reluctantly given, it motivates minimally. Research has consistently shown that job security and the quality of life in the workplace are a higher priority for most people. It is only when these internal motivators are absent that money, the most common external motivator, takes on a greater significance because, "It is the only thing we can get here, so we'll fight for every penny we can get." If money is given, received, and perceived as a

True Motivation

measure of self-worth, it does take on a much greater significance.

In the end the only truly effective motivation is internal or self-motivation, which is where the coach first comes in. Telling someone to motivate himself is a contradiction in terms. Self-motivation can be greatly enhanced by coaching and coaching can then be used to convert motivation into effective action. At this stage, telling, directing, or instructing would undermine both the motivation and the action.

The relationship between the coach and the coachee must be one of partnership in the endeavor, trust, safety, and minimal pressure. The check, the key, and the ax have no place here, as they can serve only to inhibit that relationship.

A NEW APPROACH TO MANAGEMENT

Can a Manager Be a Coach?

Can a manager, therefore, be a coach? Yes, but it demands the highest qualities of that manager: empathy, integrity, and detachment, as well as a willingness in most cases to adopt a fundamentally different approach to his staff. He will also have to find his own way, for there are few role models for him to follow. He may even have to cope with initial resistance from some of his staff, suspicious of any departure from traditional management. They may fear the additional personal responsibility implicit in a coaching style of management. These problems can be anticipated and are generally easily coached away.

The polarities of management or communication style with which we are familiar place an autocratic approach on one end of the spectrum and a laissez faire and hope for the best attitude on the other. On one end the boss feels he is in control, and knows what he has demanded, but how sure can he be that his demotivated subordinate will deliver? On the other end the subordinate, while enjoying the freedom of his own decisions, may make a decision or take an action unacceptable to his boss, even one that puts his boss at risk.

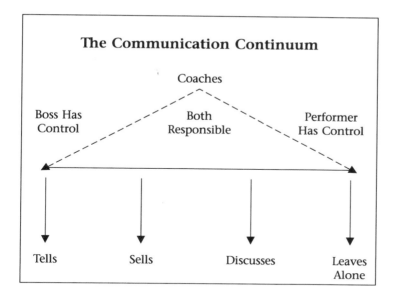

When I was a little boy, my parents told me what to do, and scolded me when I didn't do it. When I went to school, my teachers told me what to do, and disciplined me if I didn't. When I joined the army, the sergeant told me what to do, and God help me if I didn't, so I did! When I got my first job, my boss told me what to do, too. So when I reached a position of some authority, what did I do? I told people what to do, because that is what all my role models had done. That is true for the majority of us: we have been brought up on telling, and we are very good at it.

Telling

If we move along the scale to the right, we come to selling. Here the boss lays out his good idea and attempts to convince us how great it is. We know better than to challenge him, so we smile demurely and carry out his instructions. Nicer maybe, if a bit phony, and it gives the appearance of being more democratic. But is it really? We still end up doing exactly what the boss wants, and he gets little input from us. Nothing much has changed.

Selling

Discussing

When we get further along the line to discussing, resources are genuinely pooled and the good boss may be willing to follow a path other than his own option, provided it is going in the right direction. Sir John Harvey-Jones, interviewed about team leadership for David Hemery's book *Sporting Excellence,* said,

> If the direction everyone else wants is not where I thought we should go, I'll go...once the thing is rolling, you can change direction anyway. I may see they were right or they may realize it isn't the right place to be and head towards my preferred course, or we may both come to realize that we would rather be in a third alternative. In industry, you can only move with the hearts and minds.

Attractive as democratic discussion may be, it can be time consuming and result in indecision.

Leaving Alone

The right end of the scale, just leaving the subordinate to get on with it, frees the manager for other duties and gives the subordinate freedom of choice. It is, however, risky for both. The manager has abdicated his responsibility, although it still stops with him, and the subordinate may perform poorly due to a lack of awareness of many aspects of the task.

Coaching

The majority of managers will position themselves on the scale somewhere between these extremes, but coaching lies on a different plane altogether and combines the benefits of both ends with the risks of neither. Through the coaching questions and answers, the manager learns not only what actio ns the subordinate intends to take but also how he came to his conclusions. The subordinate not only is encouraged to make his own decisions but is coached to higher levels of awareness and responsibility. These two qualities are paramount to achieving and sustaining high levels of performance.

THE ROLE OF THE MANAGER

What this book is suggesting is that the left end of the scale is familiar and overused, and that further to the right lie untapped resources and a wealth of hidden potential. It is up to us to decide at each moment which is the appropriate place to be on the scale for the situation. It is seldom static and there is, therefore, no right place to remain.

What this brings up is, "What is the role of a manager?" Many managers too frequently find themselves firefighting, struggling to get the job done. By their own admission they are unable to devote the time they feel they should to long-term planning, visioning, taking the overview and surveying alternatives, the competition, new products, and so forth. Most important, they are unable to devote the time to "growing" their people, to staff development. They send their employees on a training course or two and delude themselves that this will be adequate. They seldom get their money's worth. Any trainer will agree that follow-up is essential if the lessons of training are to stick. Few companies can afford the time and the money that sufficient follow-up would demand if there were no reinforcement from within the organization, particularly the adoption of the same practices by the senior management. Few companies are willing to make such radical changes, even though their survival may depend on their doing so. However, such a culture change is not as difficult, costly, and risky as most managers might imagine. In fact, it may provide them with the very things they want.

GROWING PEOPLE

Coaching is both the tool and the essence of company culture change. A transformed organization is one in which getting the job done and growing people are given approximately equal weight. So how can managers find the time to coach their staff? It is so much quicker to tell. The paradoxical answer is that if they coach their staff, the developing staff shoulders much greater responsibility, freeing the manager from firefighting not only to coach more but also to attend to those broader issues that only he or she can address. So growing people is enlightened self-interest rather than idealism that offers no added value. Sure, at times it will be all hands to the pumps and to hell with the niceties, but that is acceptable and accepted in a culture in which people feel cared for.

The following table is frequently part of training folklore, but it is so important that it warrants repeating here.

It was a piece of research first carried out some time ago by IBM. A group of people was divided randomly into three subgroups, each of which was taught something quite simple, the same thing, using three different approaches. The results are shown in the table and they speak for themselves. One thing they reveal that particularly concerns us, however, is how dramatically recall declines when people are only *told* something.

I well remember showing this to a couple of parachutist trainers who became very concerned about the fact that they taught emergency procedures only by telling. They hurried to change their system before they were faced with a terminal freefall!

	Told	Told and Shown	Told, Shown, and Experienced
Recall after 3 weeks	70%	72%	85%
Recall after 3 months	10%	32%	65%

The Nature of Change 3

*T*he demand for change in business practice has never been greater than it is today. How has this come about? Why does what was good practice in the past not still hold good? Are we rushing into change for change's sake? How do we know it is going to be any better? And for how long? We have made all these grand changes in the past and they did not make any difference. No sooner will we have made this change than we will have to change again. Besides, what are we changing from and to? These are the anxieties of many who are threatened by the inevitable plethora of uncertainties, but they are also very valid questions, the answers to which we need to understand if we are going to manage change well.

There are many straightforward answers, such as increasing global competition forcing the pace toward leaner, more efficient, flexible, and responsive units. The pace of technological innovation leads to management frequently finding they have never learned the skills of the teams they employ. Demographic changes, the increasing integration of Europe, and the realignment and

Why Change?

refinancing of the old Eastern Bloc states all pose new challenges. There is, however, another factor—more subtle, perhaps, but so pervasive that some find it hard to identify.

A NEW AWARENESS

This factor is a growing awareness in ordinary people leading to their demand to be more involved in the decisions that affect them at work, at play, locally, nationally, or even globally. Decisions made by traditional authorities, governments, and other institutions, previously immune from challenge, are being called into question by the media, pressure groups, and concerned individuals. Isn't this what was happening within the Soviet Union and the Eastern Bloc, and what led to the collapse of communism? In our society today it is easier to get a hearing than ever before, and cracks are appearing in once-impregnable citadels' dubious respectability. Those that have something to hide hunker down and snarl, but the majority of thinking people welcome the changes, even if those changes do generate some feelings of insecurity. Whether one sees this awareness as some evolutionary emergence or merely the result of a world shrinking from immersion in a sea of instant communication, it matters not. It is upon us.

Accountability

I asked a group of senior police officers for whom I was running a coaching program to come up with a single word to describe the nature of this change that they, too, had detected. The word was "accountability." It had poignant relevance to the police at the time, but it is no less applicable in the business community. Ivan Boesky, Michael Milken, Robert Maxwell, Charles Keating, and Lloyds of London are recent examples of illicit manipulation exposed, shamed, and disposed of. Less visible perhaps, but more positive and important manifestations of the change in the air, are the various attempts being made in some segments of the business community to increase the responsibilities of their staffs.

What does *accountability* mean? To be held responsible for your actions? That sounds ominous, but would we not all like to be self-responsible? I prefer the term "responsibility" because it is proactive. Accountability is largely reactive. Accountability implies judgment. Responsibility implies choice. Choice implies freedom. Ordinary people are beginning to recognize not only that this is what they want, but also that it can be had to a greater extent than previously understood, even within our complex variety of social structures. Instead of being threatened by this, managers should realize that they can capitalize on it, give employees responsibility, and that the employees will, in turn, give their best. This way everyone wins. Evoking the coachee's choice to accept personal responsibility is a cornerstone of coaching.

Stress

There is another good reason for this. Work-related stress in the United States at least, is said to be reaching epidemic levels. A recent survey conducted by an independent research company in Minneapolis revealed that the leading cause of burnout was "little personal control allowed" in doing one's job and that this was prevalent at all times, regardless of the economy. This suggests an urgent need for change toward working practices that encourage personal responsibility.

Fear of Change

For many people, however, the fear of change—any change—looms large. This is not surprising when you consider that there is little we can do to prepare our children for the world they are inheriting. The planet certainly won't be as we have known it, but we don't know how it will be. Perhaps all we can hope to teach our children is the flexibility and adaptability to cope with what will be.

Change as the Norm

Most of what our great-grandparents taught their children would hold true throughout the young peoples' lives. They lived in a stable state, or at least stability was the accepted norm even if that was beginning to change. Most of us were brought up with that stable state mentality, but we are having to adapt to conditions that seem anything but stable. Our grandchildren will probably never know stability as we did, but they will have grown up with change as their norm, so all they will have to cope with is the varying pace of that change. We are the generation struggling to adjust to the fact that change itself is now the norm, struggling because our teeth were cut on the illusion of stability. When much of what we know and love is in flux, full acceptance of personal responsibility becomes a physical and psychological necessity for survival. We have to look after ourselves because, in a climate where *everyone* is dealing with change, nobody else will.

The Coaching Objective 4

S*ome* readers may think by now that I have departed far from the subject of coaching, and that the role of the manager and the context of change are side issues. They are not. They are the context of coaching. If they are not understood, coaching becomes merely another tool in a kit of quick fixes. It is possible to coach another person to solve a problem or to learn a new skill by diligently applying the coaching method and sequence described in this book without agreeing with the underlying coaching philosophy. The coaching may be competent and may achieve limited success, but it will fall far short of what is possible.

Some coaches have started that way. I remember one ski instructor we trained who was simply unready for the deeper understanding. His manner was authoritarian, dogmatic, and somewhat manipulative, but by systematically applying our method to skiing, he got results which, in turn, convinced him that choosing responsibility is one key to unlocking all kinds of hidden potential. He soon changed his whole philosophy on and off the slopes. Not only did he go on to write a self-coaching ski manual, and to design the best skiing program I know, he became an expert coach in the field of sales training.

RAISING AWARENESS

So far I have stressed the importance of the performer in work or sports choosing responsibility and being self-motivated. Both come from within and they cannot be imposed or enforced from the outside. Coaching is the means of generating both, but, important as they are, one more ingredient is needed to form the ground of coaching for performance. This other key element is *awareness*, which is the product of focused attention, concentration, and clarity. The *Concise Oxford Dictionary* defines *aware* as "conscious, not ignorant, having knowledge." I prefer what Webster adds: "aware implies having knowledge of something through alertness in observing or in interpreting what one sees, hears, feels, etc." Like our eyesight or our hearing, both of which can be keen or poor, there are infinite degrees of awareness. Unlike eyesight or hearing, in which the norm is good, the norm of our everyday awareness is rather poor. A magnifying glass or an amplifier can raise our sight and hearing threshold way above normal. In the same way, awareness can be heightened considerably by focused attention and by practice. Increased awareness gives greater clarity of perception than normal, as does a magnifying glass.

While awareness includes seeing and hearing in the workplace, it encompasses much more. It is the gathering and the clear perception of the relevant facts and information, and the ability to determine what is relevant. That ability will include an understanding of systems, dynamics, relationships between things and people, and inevitably some understanding of psychology. Awareness also encompasses self-awareness, in particular recognizing *when* and *how* emotions or desires distort one's own perception.

In the development of physical skills, the awareness of body sensations may be crucial. In the majority of sports, for example, the most effective way to increase individual physical efficiency is for the performer to become increasingly aware of the physical sensations during an activity. This is poorly understood by the majority of sports coaches, who persist in imposing their technique from *outside*. When kinesthetic awareness is focused on a movement, the immediate discomforts and corresponding inefficiencies in the movement are reduced and soon eliminated. The result is a more fluid and efficient form that corresponds more closely to the "book" technique, with the important advantage that it is geared to the particular performer's body rather than the "average" body that the book addresses.

Each activity is geared to different parts of ourselves. Sports are primarily physical, but some sports are highly visual, too. Musicians require and develop high levels of auditory awareness. Sculptors and magicians need tactile awareness, and businesspeople primarily use mental awareness.

Though all this explanation of awareness may at first seem daunting, it is something that develops quickly through simple practice and application, and through being coached. It is perhaps easier to relate to the following lay definitions:

- Awareness is knowing what is happening around you.
- Self-awareness is knowing what you are experiencing.

Awareness Leads to Skill

Awareness and *responsibility* are, without doubt, two qualities that are crucial to performance in any activity. Olympic gold medalist, David Hemery, researched sixty-three of the world's top performers from more than twenty different sports for his book, *Sporting Excellence*. In spite of considerable variations in other areas, awareness and responsibility consistently appeared to be the two most important attitudinal factors common to all— and the attitude or the state of mind of the performer is the key to performance of any kind.

Awareness and Responsibility

The Mind Is Key

For his research, David asked each of the performers to what extent they thought the mind was involved in playing their sport. He wrote, "The unanimous verdict was couched in words like 'immensely,' 'totally,' 'that's the whole game,' 'you play with your mind,' 'that's where the body movement comes from.' And as a minimum, 'It's equal to the body.'" Top performance in business demands no less. The mind is key.

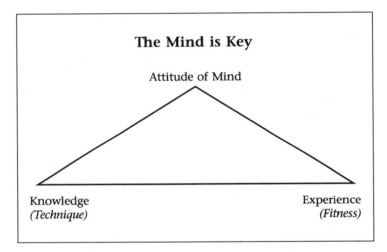

The Mind is Key

Attitude of Mind

Knowledge
(*Technique*)

Experience
(*Fitness*)

Knowledge and experience may be the business equivalents of sporting technique and physical fitness. Neither guarantees a place at the top, and many successful people have proved that neither is indispensable. A winning mind is essential.

The Winning Mind

A decade or so ago technical ability and fitness commensurate with your sport were what coaches worked on. The mind was not universally recognized to be so crucial, but that was what the performer was born with, and the coach could not do much about it. Wrong! Coaches could and did affect the state of mind of their performers, but largely unwittingly and often negatively by their autocratic methods and obsession with technique.

Coaches denied their performers' responsibility by telling them what to do; they denied their awareness by telling them what they saw. They withheld responsibility and killed awareness. Some coaches still do, as do many managers. They contribute to the performers' or employees' limitations as well as to their successes. The problem is that they may still get reasonable results from those they manage, so they are not motivated to try anything else, and never know or believe what they could achieve by other means.

Recently much has changed in sports and most top teams employ sports psychologists to provide performers with attitudinal training. If old coaching methods remain unchanged, however, the coach will frequently be unintentionally negating the psychologist's efforts. The best way to develop and maintain the ideal state of mind for performance is to build awareness and responsibility continuously throughout the daily practice and the skill-acquisition process. This requires a shift in the method of coaching, a shift from instruction to real coaching.

The parallels in business are not hard to see. The mind is key, and the management methodology chosen will either enhance or inhibit the minds of the managed. The choice is ours.

INTERNAL OR SELF-MOTIVATION

The secret of motivation is the Holy Grail that every business leader would love to find. Self-motivation is, of course, all in the mind and that is no secret. We know that the mind is key, but where is the key to the mind? Motivation would also appear easier to come by in sports than it is in business, although many sports-people and their coaches are also seeking more.

In Sport

Sports are usually more fun and the external rewards are more immediate, more glamorous, and, at the top, often richer in fortune and fame. More important, however, sports performances, at all levels, are ultimately, exclusively in the hands of the performers (total responsibility). In addition, the choice to take up a sport, any sport, is often driven by the desire for self-worth and identity. This constitutes a large measure of self-motivation. Now we have all the winning ingredients.

In Business

The time-scale in business is far longer, the fun quotient is questionable for the majority, and there is precious little glamour beyond the deluxe version of the company car. Even the big financial harvests generally only accrue to the few.

What cues to motivation remain then in business? There are clearly three internal motivators:

- The opportunity for real responsibility and choice.
- The opportunity to build self-esteem and identity.
- The opportunity to experience a sense of making a real contribution, a desire for which lurks within us all.

The first two cues are readily available in businesses of all kinds and at all levels in the hierarchy, provided the business follows the principles from which coaching stems, and providing that coaching is the management style employed. The external component of these two is promotion, but much of the time that is not possible or frequent, making the internal component indispensable.

The third is a big issue beyond the scope of our subject and will depend on the values, ethics, and breadth of vision of each individual. However, anyone working on profit-only projects and products that conflict with their own values will experience inner conflict, which when suppressed, may cause their work and even their health to suffer.

A couple of examples will illustrate the point. However you may judge the activities of Greenpeace, I suggest that motivation is not a major problem for its members. For other such organizations, it may not be quite so straightforward. At Oxfam, the British charitable agency for whom I coached on occasion, the idealism of the wider vision that attracted most of their staff became easily submerged by preoccupation with all the problems of running a chain of 800 or more small shops. Field workers are unfortunately in a minority. The challenge for Oxfam's management was how to ensure that all the staff could share the vision and its motivating impact even though the daily activities were uninspiring by nature and the pay was low.

Once again a company that offers its staff real responsibility and opportunities for building self-worth will have little trouble motivating them. This means developing a coaching culture. See Chapter 12 for an example of this.

Effective Questions 5

If we accept that the coaching objective is to raise awareness and responsibility, how do we do this? Contrary to the belief of a surprising number of people, telling people to be aware and to be responsible does not work. If anything it generates resistance, often in the form of irritated spoken or unspoken responses such as, "I am," "I know," "Of course," or "What do you think I'm doing?"

"Watch the ball!" is the number-one instruction in tennis, but it invariably irritates the player and only produces an improvement for a ball or two. "Watch the ball, I said. How many times do I have to tell you to *watch the ball?*" It is all so predictable.

But if the coach were to ask you "Which way does the ball spin as it crosses the net?" "How high over the net is it this time?" or "Can you see the point of contact between the ball and the racket?" or "How many times do you see the maker's name on the ball after it

Watch the Ball

29

bounces?" what would you do? Yes, in order to answer the question, you would have to look at the ball and you would go on looking at the ball so long as new questions were coming. You are even likely to become so fascinated with the new awareness you have found that you will continue to focus on the ball long after the questions have ceased.

Ask, Don't Tell

It is the question that focuses the attention and increases the awareness, not the much more limited command to "watch the ball." It is also questions that focus the attention and evoke clarity in business. "What is current stock?" "What is the most difficult issue for you?" "When is the engineer going to arrive?" All these are specific questions that demand specific answers.

In tennis, learning to focus attention on the ball alone is often enough to cause a considerable performance improvement. So it is in business, where seeing things with greater clarity alone is likely to cause people to take more timely and effective action and therefore to improve their performance.

If I wish to increase someone's responsibility or ownership of a task, I could just say, "You are responsible for this" or "You do this." But does that make you feel truly responsible? No, it contains a veiled threat, so you will try to do it to keep out of trouble. But what if you do it and it does not work? "I did exactly what you said but..." or "I knew it wouldn't work doing it that way" or even, "I told you so" will be your retort.

How much better it would be if I were to ask a question or two instead. "Who will take on this one?" "How confident do you feel that you can complete this on time?" "Is there any element of this that you are unsure of?" "Can you see any obstacles to achieving this?" "When can you have it done?" All these questions generate responsibility and ownership, but they also raise awareness of other factors too.

These examples are probably sufficient to convince you that awareness and responsibility are raised better by asking than by telling. It follows, therefore, that the primary form of verbal interaction from a good coach is in the interrogative. Now we need to examine what the most effective kinds of questions are.

We most commonly ask questions in order to elicit information. I may require information to resolve an issue for myself, or if I am proffering advice or a solution to someone else. If I am a coach, however, the answers are of secondary importance. The information is not for me to use and may not have to be complete. I only need to know that the coachee has the necessary information. The coachee's answers frequently indicate to the coach the line to follow with subsequent questions, while at the same time enable him to monitor whether the coachee is following a productive track, or one that is in line with the purpose or company objectives.

The Function of Questions

The most effective questions for raising awareness and responsibility begin with words that seek to *quantify*, words like *what*, *when*, *who*, *how much*, and *how many*. *Why* is discouraged because it often implies criticism and evokes defensiveness, and *why* and *how*, if unqualified, both cause analytical thinking, which can be counter-productive. Analysis (thinking) and awareness (observation) are dissimilar mental modes which are virtually impossible to employ simultaneously. If the accurate reporting of facts is called for, analysis of their importance and meaning is better temporarily suspended. *Why* questions are better expressed as, "What were the reasons...?" and *how* questions as, "What are the steps...?" They evoke more specific, factual answers.

Interrogative Words

Questions should begin broadly and increasingly focus on detail. This demand for more detail maintains the focus and the interest of the performer. The point is well illustrated by the exercise of looking at a square foot of carpet. After observing the pile, color, pattern, and perhaps a spot or a stain, the carpet will hold little further interest for the observer and his attention will begin to wander to more interesting things. Give him a magnifying glass and he will look again in greater depth and for a longer period of time before becoming bored. A microscope could turn that little piece of carpet into a fascinating universe of forms, textures, colors, microbes, and

Focus on Detail

even live bugs, all sufficient to transfix the eye and mind of the observer for many minutes more.

So it is in business coaching. The coach needs to probe deeper or for more detail to keep the coachee involved and to bring into his consciousness those often partially obscured factors that may be important.

Areas of Interest

How, then, does the coach determine what aspects of an issue are important, especially if it is in an area about which he is not particularly knowledgeable? The principle is that questions should follow the interest and the train of thought of the coachee, not of the coach. This is important, if a little controversial, and will be elaborated on in Chapter 6. Paradoxically it may also be valuable for the coach to focus on any aspect that the coachee appears to be avoiding. So as not to break the trust and the responsibility of the coachee, this avenue of exploration is best entered into by a statement followed by a question: "I notice that you have not mentioned.... Is there any particular reason for this?"

Blind Spots

Golfers and tennis players might be interested in the physical parallel to this principle. A coach might ask a pupil which part of his swing or stroke he finds most difficult to feel or be accurately aware of. It is most likely that in this "blind spot" lies a suppressed discomfort or flaw in the movement. As the coach seeks more and more awareness in that area, the feeling is restored and the correction occurs naturally without resort to technical input from the coach. The curative properties of awareness are legion!

Open Questions

Finally, *open* questions requiring descriptive answers promote awareness whereas *closed* questions are too absolute for accuracy, and *yes* or *no* answers close the door on the exploration of further detail. Open questions are much more effective for generating awareness and responsibility in the coaching process.

The Role of the Coach 6

The coach is not a problem solver, a teacher, an advisor, an instructor, or even an expert; he or she is a sounding board, a facilitator, a counselor, an awareness raiser. These words should help you to understand what the role implies.

QUALITIES OF A COACH

In our coaching courses we ask participants to list the qualities that an ideal coach would possess. The following is a typical list and one with which I agree:

- Patience
- Detachment
- Supportive attitude
- Interest
- Good listener
- Perceptive

- Aware
- Self-aware
- Attentive
- Retentive

Often the list also contains some of the following:

- Technical expertise
- Knowledge
- Experience
- Credibility
- Authority

Coach as Expert

I am less in agreement with these and I pose a question: Does a coach need to have experience or technical knowledge in the area in which he or she is coaching? The answer is no—not if the coach is truly acting as a detached awareness raiser. If, however, the coach does not fully believe in what he espouses, i.e. the potential of the performer and the value of self-responsibility, then he will think that he needs expertise in the subject to be able to coach. I am not suggesting that there is never a place for expert input, but the less-skilled coach will tend to overuse it and thereby reduce the value of his coaching, because every time input is provided, the responsibility of the coachee is reduced.

The Pitfalls of Knowledge

The ideal would seem to be an expert coach with a wealth of technical knowledge, too. It is, however, very hard for experts to withhold their expertise sufficiently to coach well. Let me illustrate this further with an example from tennis. Many years ago several of our Inner Tennis courses were so popular that we ran out of trained Inner Tennis coaches. We brought in two Inner Ski coaches, dressed them in tennis coaches' uniforms, put rackets under their arms, and let them loose with the promise that they would not attempt to use the racket under any circumstances.

Not entirely to our surprise, the coaching job they performed was largely indistinguishable from that of their tennis-playing colleagues. However, on a couple of notable occasions they actually did *better*. On reflection the reason became clear. The tennis coaches were seeing the participants in terms of their technical faults; the ski coaches, who could not recognize such faults, saw the participants in terms of the efficiency with which they used their bodies. Body inefficiency stems from self-doubt and inadequate body awareness. The ski coaches were therefore tackling problems at cause, whereas the tennis coaches were only tackling the symptoms, the technical faults. This obliged us to do more training with the tennis coaches to enable them to better detach themselves from their expertise.

A Level Deeper

Let's look at the same thing with a simple example from a business context. A manager saw that her subordinate, George, did not communicate sufficiently with his colleagues in the next department, and knew that a weekly progress memo was the solution. Such a memo, however, would contain inadequate information so long as George's resistance to communicating with them persisted. Instead of being satisfied with George's agreement to send memos, the manager coached George to discover and let go of his own resistance. The lack of communication was the symptom, but the resistance was the cause. Problems can only be resolved at the level beneath that at which they manifest.

The Manager — Expert or Coach?

It is hard, but by no means impossible, for an expert to be a good coach. Of course, the expertise is invaluable for many other aspects of a manager's function, and the truth is that the manager is most likely an expert anyway. But take the case of a senior manager in an organization that computerizes a part of its operations. If he is a good coach, then he should have no difficulty coaching his staff to further develop their computer skills, whether he understands the new system or not. As soon as he does this, any credibility gap that may exist in the minds of some of his staff will soon disappear, which enables him to retain command of that department. As skills become more specialized and technically complex, coaching may be an absolute prerequisite for managers.

Leading Questions

We can now look at what we might call the purely facilitative aspect of coaching, beginning with the asking of questions. They need to be asked in a calm, noncritical tone of voice. Leading questions, the resort of many poor coaches, indicate that the coach does not believe in what he is attempting to do. It will be quickly recognized by the coachee, and trust and the value of the coaching session will be reduced. Better for the coach to tell the coachee that he has a suggestion rather than attempt to manipulate the coachee in that direction. Also, questions that imply criticism should be avoided, such as, "Why on earth did you do that?"

Follow Coachee's Interest

Questions should follow the interest of the coachee. If the coach leads the direction of the questions, he will undermine the responsibility of the coachee. But what if the direction in which he is going is a dead end or a distraction? Trust that the coachee will soon find that out for himself. If coachees are not allowed to explore avenues in which they have an interest, the fascination is likely to persist and cause distortions or diversions in the work itself, rather than merely in the coaching session. Once coachees have explored their interests, they will be far more present and focused on whatever will emerge as the best path.

Be Attentive to Answers

The coach must be fully attentive to coachees' answers to questions. Trust will be lost if he isn't, additionally he will not know the best question to ask next. It must be a spontaneous process. Questions prepared in the mind prior to the time of asking will disrupt the flow and not follow the interest of the coachee. If the coach is working out the next question while the coachee is speaking, the coachee will be aware that the coach is not really listening. Far better to hear them through and then pause, if necessary, while the next appropriate question comes to mind.

Most people are not good at listening to others; we are told to listen at school, not trained or coached to listen. It is a skill that requires concentration and practice. Yet, strangely enough, few people have difficulty listening to the news or to their favorite TV show. Interest holds the attention; perhaps we need to learn to be interested in others. It is greatly appreciated when we really listen to someone, or when someone really listens to us. When we listen, do we *really* hear? When we look, do we *really* see? We shortchange ourselves and those we coach if we do not really hear and see them, meaning we maintain eye contact with them. Preoccupation with our own thoughts and opinions and the compulsion to talk, particularly if one is placed in any kind of advisory role, is strong. It has been said that because we were given two ears and one mouth, we should listen twice as much as we speak! Perhaps the hardest thing a coach has to learn to do is to shut up.

Tone of Voice

What do we listen to and for? The coachee's tone of voice will indicate any emotion and should be listened to. A monotone may indicate repetition of an old line of thought, while a more animated voice will indicate the awakening of new ideas. The coachee's choice of words can be very revealing: a predominance of negative terms, a shift toward formality or childish language—all have hidden meaning that can help the coach to understand and therefore facilitate effectively.

Body Language

In addition to listening, the coach needs to watch the coachee's body language, not with the purpose of making glib observations but, again, to help with the choice of question. The coachee's high interest level in the direction of the coaching may well be indicated by a forward posture. Uncertainty or anxiety in answers may be revealed by his hand partially covering his mouth while speaking. Arms folded across the chest often indicate resistance or defiance, and an open body posture suggests receptivity and flexibility. I am not going to go into the many aspects of body language here, but one guide is that if the words say one thing and the body seems to be saying something else, the body is more likely to indicate the true feelings.

Reflecting Back

So there are listening, hearing, watching, and understanding, and the coach needs to be self-aware enough to know which she is doing. However clear the coach may feel, it is worth reflecting back to the coachee from time to time and summarizing points. This will ensure correct understanding and reassure the coachee that he is being fully heard and understood. It also gives him a second chance to check on the veracity of what he has said. It is recommended that the coach take notes during the coaching session, for this reason and others I will state later.

Self-awareness

Finally, the good coach will be applying self-awareness to carefully monitor his reactions, of emotion or judgment, to any of the coachee's responses, including those to the coachee personally, that might interfere with the necessary objectivity and detachment of the coach. Our own psychological history and prejudices—and no one is free of either—will influence our communication.

Projection and Transference

Projection and *transference* are the psychological distortions that all those who teach, guide, coach, or manage others need to learn to recognize and minimize. Projection means projecting onto another person one's own positive or negative traits or qualities. Transference is "the displacement of patterns of feelings and behavior, originally experienced with significant figures of one's childhood, to individuals in one's current relationships." In the workplace one of the most common manifestations of this is authority transference.

In any hierarchical relationship, manager/subordinate or even coach/coachee, both parties' issues or unconscious feelings about authority will be operating. For example, many people give away their power to the designated authority—"he knows, has all the answers, is more advanced," etc.—and make themselves small and childlike. This might serve the wishes of an authoritarian manager for dominance and dependency on him, but it works against the objective of coaching, which is to generate responsibility in the people managed.

Another common example of an unconscious transference reaction to authority is that of rebellion and covert sabotage of the work goals. Individual transference will increase the collective frustrations and feelings of powerlessness wherever management style limits choice. One major automaker used to be able to assess the state of labor relations from the percentage of good parts dumped into the reject bins alongside the assembly line.

Countertransference

Countertransference, which is a further complication of transference, occurs when the person in authority, manager or coach, herself unconsciously reacts to the transference from her own history by perpetuating the dependence or the rebellion. A good manager or coach will recognize her potential for this and compensate for the effects of all manifestations of transference by consciously working to empower the subordinate or coachee. If she does not, these distortions will creep into managerial or coaching relationships with the long-term effect of seriously undermining her management style.

The Sequence of 7
Questioning

S*o* far we have established the essential nature of
awareness and responsibility for learning and for
performance improvement. We have looked at the context of coaching, at the parallels between coaching and
managing, and at company culture and change. We have
explored the role and the attitude of the coach, and we
have considered questions as his primary form of communication. We now have to determine what to ask
questions about, and in what sequence to ask them.

Formal or Informal?

It is important to stress that coaching can be loose and
informal, so much so that the coachee does not know
she is being coached. For the everyday management
function of briefing and debriefing staff, nothing is
better than coaching, but it should not be identified as
such; it would just be managing. In this case coaching
ceases to be a tool of management and simply becomes
the way to manage people—in my opinion, the most
effective way. At the other end of the spectrum, a

coaching session can be scheduled and structured in such a way that the purpose and the roles are straightforward. While the majority of coaching is of the former type, we will examine the latter in detail because, while the process is the same, the stages are more sharply defined.

THE FUNDAMENTALS OF COACHING

For reasons of simplicity and clarity, we will look at one-to-one coaching, although the format of team coaching or even self-coaching remains exactly the same. Both of these will be elaborated on in later chapters. One-to-one coaching may take place between peers, between a manager and a subordinate, between a former teacher and a student, between a coach and a performer, or between a counselor and someone seeking their assistance. One-to-one coaching can even be used in an upward direction—although generally covertly—by an employee on his boss. After all, as no one gets very far by telling his boss what to do, coaching upward has a much higher success rate!

The sequence of questions I suggest would follow four distinct headings:

- *Goal* setting for the session, short-term as well as long-term.
- *Reality* checking to explore the current situation.
- *Options* and alternative strategies, or courses of action.
- *What* is to be done, *when*, by *whom* and the *will* to do it.

This conveniently forms the mnemonic *GROW*, to which I will refer frequently and which is used in the subtitle of this book. I must stress, however, and I will repeat often, that GROW, without the context of awareness and responsibility and the skill of questioning to generate them, has little value. Mnemonics abound in the training business. There is SPIN, there are SMART goals...and there is GROW. Mnemonics are occasionally presented or misperceived as panaceas to all business ills.

They are nothing of the sort; they are only as valuable as the context in which they are used, and the context of GROW is awareness and responsibility. An authoritative boss might charge his employees in the following way:

My *goal* is to sell one thousand widgets this month.

The *reality* is that you did poorly last month and only sold 400. You are a bunch of lazy good-for-nothings. Our principle competitor has a better product, so you have to try harder.

I have considered all the *options* and we are not going to increase our advertising or repackage the product.

What you *will* do is the following....

He has followed the GROW model to the letter but he did not ask a single question. He created no awareness and, although he thinks he has threatened his staff into taking responsibility, this is not so, because they had no choice.

Context and Flexibility

If you get anything at all out of this book, let it be awareness and responsibility, not GROW. Having said that, the strongest case for following the GROW sequence with effective coaching questions is that it works.

It is, however, subject to recycling. One may only be able to define a vague goal until one has examined the reality in some detail. It will then be necessary to go back and define the goal much more precisely before moving forward again. Even a sharply defined initial goal may be recognized as wrong or inappropriate once the reality is clear.

When listing the *options,* it will be necessary to check back to see if each of them would, in fact, move you toward the desired goal. Finally, before the *what* and *when* are set in concrete, it is crucial to make a final check to see if they meet the goal.

We will now take a deeper look at each one of these steps in turn and at the questions that best raise awareness and responsibility within each step.

Goal Setting   8

*S*o much has been written about the importance and the process of goal setting that there is certainly no need for me to repeat it all in a book about coaching. Goal setting could fill a book on its own. However, I hope those who consider themselves to be goal-setting experts will forgive me if I review those aspects of goal setting that we consider especially important for the coaching process.

We would invariably begin a coaching session by determining a goal for the session itself. If the coachee has sought a session, clearly it is he who needs to define what he wants to get from it. Even if it is the coach or manager who has requested the session to resolve a specific issue that he spells out, the coachee can still be asked whether there is anything else that he wants from the session.

The coach could ask questions like the following:

- What would you like to get out of this session?
- I have half an hour for this, where would you like to have gotten by then?

The Goal for the Session

- What would be the most helpful thing for you to take away from this session?

These questions would elicit answers like the following:

- An outline for the month that I can develop.
- A clear idea of and commitment to my next two action steps.
- A decision as to which way to jump.
- An understanding of the principle issues.
- An agreed budget for the job.

The Goal for the Issue

Now we come to the goal or goals related to the issue at hand and here we need to be able to distinguish *end* goals from *performance* goals.

An End Goal

The final objective—to become the market leaders, to be appointed sales director, to land the ICI account, to win the gold medal—is seldom absolutely within one's own control. You cannot know or control what your competitors will do.

A Performance Goal

The identification of the performance level that you believe will provide you a very good chance of achieving the end goal. It is largely within your control and it generally provides a means of measuring progress. Examples of performance goals might be for 95 percent of production to pass quality control the first time, for us to sell 100 widgets next month, or to have run the mile in 4 minutes, 10 seconds by the end of September.

It is far easier to commit yourself to—and take responsibility for—a performance goal, which is within your control, than an end goal, which is not. An end goal should, wherever possible, be supported by a performance goal. The end goal may provide the inspiration, but the performance goal defines the specification.

Performance Goals Are Crucial

The lack of an established performance goal played a major role in a notorious upset for Britain in the 1968 Olympics. Welshman Lynn Davies had won the gold medal in the long jump in 1964 and Davies, Igor Ter-ovanesyan, a Russian, and Ralph Boston, the American champion, were expected to share the medals. Along came a very erratic American, Bob Beamon, who, in the very first round, jumped some two feet beyond the world record. When one considers that the world record had risen by only six inches since 1936, this truly was a prodigious feat. Davies, Boston, and Ter-ovanesyan were all completely demoralized, and, although Boston got the bronze and Ter-ovanesyan was fourth, both were six inches behind their best jumps. Davies, who was a foot behind his best, admits he was only focused on the gold, and that if he had set himself a performance goal of, say, twenty-seven feet, or a personal best, and had kept going for *that,* he would have won the silver.

OWNERSHIP OF GOALS

Although company directors may be free to set their own goals, all too often they pass goals down the line as imperatives not to be questioned. This denies ownership to those who are expected to meet these targets and their performance is likely to suffer accordingly. Wise directors will strive to maintain a healthy detachment from their own goals when they are seeking to motivate their managers and will always encourage them to set their own challenging goals whenever feasible. But if they don't do this and a job is tightly proscribed, all is not totally lost, for the production manager may at least be able to offer his staff some choice and ownership of *how* a job is done, *who* does *what,* and *when.*

Even if a certain goal is an absolute imperative, it is still possible to coach for ownership. I was recently discussing firearms training with a county police force. How would it be possible to have trainees own the absolute, inflexible rules of firearms safety, they asked. I suggested

Coaching for Ownership

that instead of presenting them with these rules at the outset, they should have a discussion, using coaching, out of which the trainees would create their own agreed set of safety rules. The chances are that it would closely parallel the institutional ones. Where they were at variance, the reasons for the variation, with minimal input from the tutor, could be coached out of the trainees. This way the trainees would have a far greater degree of appreciation, understanding, and ownership of the institutional firearms safety rules.

Whose Goal?

Never underestimate the value of choice and responsibility in terms of self-motivation. For example, if a sales team comes up with a goal that is lower than the boss wishes, the boss should consider the consequences very carefully before overriding the team's figure and imposing his own. He may do better to swallow his pride and accept their figure. Imposing his own figure may have the effect of lowering the performance of the team, even though his target was higher than theirs. They may or may not consider his figure discouragingly unrealistic, but they will certainly be demotivated by their lack of choice. Of course, the boss has one more option if he is sure of his ground, and that is to start with the team's figure and coach them upward by exploring and helping them to dismantle their barriers to achieving more. The team then retains responsibility for attaining the final figure.

Qualities of a Good Goal

It is not only important to support end goals with performance goals, but also with goals that are SMART:

- Specific
- Measurable
- Attainable
- Realistic
- Time-phased

and PURE

- Positively stated
- Understood
- Relevant
- Ethical

and CLEAR

- Challenging
- Legal
- Environmentally sound
- Agreed upon
- Recorded

The point of a goal having most of these qualities should be self-evident, but a couple of observations may be in order.

If a goal is not *attainable*, there is no hope, but if it is not *challenging*, there is no motivation. So there is an envelope here into which all goals should fit.

It is very important to state goals in the *positive*. What happens if a goal is stated in the negative, for example, we must not remain at the bottom of the regional sales league. What is the attention focused on? Being at the bottom of the league, of course! If I say to you, "Don't think about a red balloon," what comes to mind? Or if I say to a child, "Don't drop that glass, spill the water, or make a mistake"? Consider this example from baseball. As a batter leaves the dugout, some joker says to him, "Don't swing at any bad pitches." The batter has the long walk to the batter's box to think about swinging at a bad pitch...and so he does.

Negative goals can easily be converted to the positive, for example, "We are going to finish fourth in the league, or higher" or "I am going to resist taking the first pitch, no matter how tempting it may be to swing."

Goals must be *agreed on* between all parties involved: the boss who thinks he ought to set them, the sales

State Goals in the Positive

manager, and the team who has to do the job. Without agreement, the vital ownership and responsibility of the sales team is lost, and their performance will suffer accordingly.

It may sound like preaching to suggest that goals should be *legally*, *ethically*, and *environmentally sound*, but each individual has his or her own personal code about these things and the only way to ensure employees' full alignment is to conform to the highest standards. Besides, the new accent on accountability in business and throughout society, and the consequences of exposure by a whistle-blower or a consumer watchdog, surely outweigh any short-term gain that may tempt the unscrupulous! In *Sporting Excellence*, David Hemery quotes Sir Michael Edwardes as saying:

> You will not get the TOP people working with you unless you have the highest standards of business integrity. If you value what you get out of corner cutting at $1,000, the damage you do in demotivation of good people is minus $20,000.

Some effort may be necessary to ensure that all goals are clearly *understood*, for too often inaccurate assumptions distort some people's perception, even of goals they have taken part in creating.

Olympic Goal

Perhaps the most striking example of good and successful goal setting I know of comes from the Olympics. A college freshman named John Nabor watched Mark Spitz win an extraordinary seven gold medals for swimming in the 1972 Olympics in Munich. There and then John decided that he would win the gold in the 100-meter backstroke in 1976. Although he had won the National Junior Championship at the time, he was still nearly five seconds off the pace required to win the Olympics. That is a huge amount to make up at that age and over such a short swimming distance.

He decided to make the impossible possible first by setting himself a performance goal of a new world record, and then by dividing his five-second deficit by the number of hours of training he could muster in four years.

He calculated that he had to improve his time by one-fifth of an eyeblink for every hour of training, and he felt that was possible if he worked intelligently as well as hard. It was possible. He had improved so much by 1976 that he was made captain of the American swimming team for Montreal. He also won the gold medal in both the 100-meter and the 200-meter backstroke, the first in world-record time, and the second as an Olympic record. Good goal setting! John Nabor was motivated by a clearly defined *end* goal, which he supported with a *performance* goal that was within his control. He bolstered this with a systematic *process* and this formed the dais on which he was to stand.

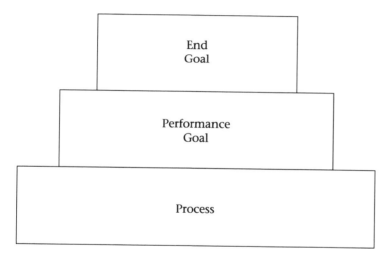

A SAMPLE COACHING SESSION

Throughout the four chapters covering each segment of the coaching sequence, I will illustrate the points made with the dialogue of a fictional coaching session with Joe Butter. Joe is a senior accounts manager in a New York advertising agency. His early meteoric rise through the ranks has slowed in the last two years, coinciding with the onset of his middle age and the increase in his intake of food and drink, resulting in the expansion of his waistline. Recently he tried to cut back and began exercising, but he was plagued by boredom, failure, excuses, guilt, and lack of commitment. He shares his concern with a colleague, Mike, who offers to coach him on it.

Mike:	Ok, Joe, what would you like to have by the end of this half hour?
Joe:	Some kind of plan to get in better shape.
Mike:	For the rest of your life, or what?
Joe:	No, that would be too tall an order, and besides, it might change once I get going. A realistic program for three months would be great.
Mike:	Let's look long-term for a moment. What is the purpose of getting fit for you?
Joe:	I'm just feeling lousy about myself, and my work is suffering. I want to feel good again.
Mike:	Fine. How fit would you like to be and by when?
Joe:	I would like to lose fifteen pounds or so. And within a few months, I would like to be able not only to run upstairs and run for the train without getting out of breath, but also I would actually like to enjoy running.
Mike:	Exactly what weight do you want to get down to, and by what date?
Joe:	210 pounds by the end of the summer; that's about fifteen pounds I have to lose.
Mike:	What day exactly?
Joe:	By September 20.
Mike:	Today is February 19, so that gives you seven months.
Joe:	Hmmm...two pounds a month, or maybe it will go faster to begin with.
Mike:	What do you want to lose by June 1?
Joe:	Ten pounds by then.
Mike:	You could do that by not eating and yet not be much fitter. How can we measure fitness?
Joe:	I'll run 20 miles a week from the beginning of September onward.
Mike:	Any particular speed?

Joe: No, I'll be happy to do it at all, and I'll know if I'm doing it satisfactorily.

Mike: I don't care what speed, Joe, just give yourself a target speed. What will it be?

Joe: OK, nine-minute miles.

Joe now has a goal for the session, a long-term goal and a halfway mark. His goals are specific, measurable, and probably incorporate all the qualities we recommend. Because there are no corporate imperatives in this case, he has complete and total responsibility for his own goals. Now it is time to take a look at *reality*.

What Is Reality? 9

*N**ow* that we've defined various goals, we need to clarify the current situation. It can be argued that goals cannot be established until the current situation is known and understood, and that we should begin with *reality*. I reject this argument on the basis that a purpose is essential to give value and direction to any discussion. Even if goals can be only loosely defined before the situation is looked at in some detail, this needs to be done first. Then, when the reality is clear, the goals can be brought into sharper focus or even altered if the situation turns out to be a little different from what was previously thought.

BE OBJECTIVE

The most important criterion for examining reality is objectivity. Objectivity is subject to major distortions caused by the opinions, judgments, expectations, prejudices, concerns, hopes, and fears of the perceiver. Awareness is perceiving things as they *really* are; self-awareness is recognizing those internal factors that distort one's own perception of reality. Most people think that they are objective, but absolute objectivity does not exist. The best we have is degrees of it, but the closer we manage to get to it, the better.

Detachment

To approach *reality*, then, the potential distortions of both the coach and the coachee must be bypassed. This demands a high degree of detachment on the part of the coach, and the ability to phrase questions in a way that demands factual answers of the coachee. "What were the factors that determined your decision?" will evoke a more accurate response than "Why did you do that?" which tends to produce what the coachee believes the coach wishes to hear, or a defensive justification.

Description, Not Judgment

The coach should use—and, as much as possible, encourage the coachee to use—descriptive rather than evaluative terminology. This helps to maintain detachment and objectivity and reduces the counterproductive self-criticism that distorts perception. The diagram that follows perhaps best illustrates the point.

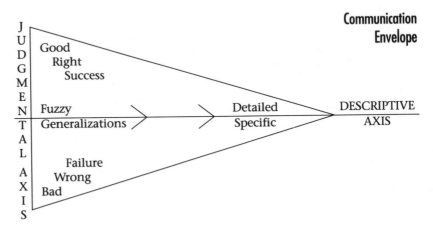

The terminology used in normal conversation, and many managerial interactions, generally falls to the left end on the descriptive axis. In coaching we try to move to the right. The more specific and descriptive our words and phrases become, the less criticism they tend to carry, and the more productive the coaching will be.

Care should be taken to remain close to the horizontal axis as often as possible. After all, there is not much I can do with the knowledge that my presentation was *bad*, but if I receive feedback that it was clearly structured, monotonic, brief, colorfully illustrated, and beneath the knowledge level of the audience, I am in a much better position to make improvements. Of course, some words, like colors or dimensions, are purely descriptive; others acquire a vertical value only when some ideal is agreed on. Yet others contain within them a degree of value in most usage (words such as "lively" or "weak"); but some are essentially evaluative, like "good and bad" or "right and wrong." So, don't just tell a marksman that he missed—that will only make him feel bad. He wants to know that his shot was one-half inch above the bull's-eye and one-quarter inch to the right if he is to make the correction. Description adds value; criticism usually detracts value.

Reality questions, when applied to self, provide the most straightforward means of self-assessment. More about this and the way it can be applied for self-development is given in Chapter 13, but the skill of asking effective reality questions is paramount, whatever the application.

Follow the Coachee

The good coach will be inclined to follow the interest or chain of thought of the coachee, while, at the same time, monitoring how that relates to the subject as a whole. Only when the coachee is ready to leave each aspect of the issue should the coach raise anything that he deems to have been omitted. If the coachee seems to have wandered far off the track, a question like, "In what way does this relate to the problem?" may bring him back or reveal a valid reason for his detour. Either way, it allows him to continue to lead the process.

Use the Senses

In most business-coaching scenarios, the reality will concern the facts and figures, the incidents that occurred, the actions taken, the obstacles to be overcome, the resources and people available, and so on—things called up by and from the mind. However, if the coachee is learning a new physical skill, such as operating a tool of his trade, from a train engine to a tennis racket, the coaching will also be focused on the senses: touch, hearing, and sight.

Body awareness brings with it automatic self-correction. If at first this seems hard to believe, just close your eyes for a moment and focus your attention internally on your facial muscles. You will probably notice a furrowed brow or a tight jaw. Almost simultaneous with that awareness, you are likely to experience a letting go, after which the brow or the jaw will be fully relaxed. The same principle applies to a complex physical movement. If attention is focused internally on the moving parts, the efficiency-reducing tensions will be felt, and automatically released, resulting in an improved performance. This is the basis of the new coaching approach to sporting technique and proficiency. Internal awareness increases body efficiency, which, in turn, results in improved technique. It is technique from the inside out rather than from the outside in. Furthermore, it is technique-owned, integrated, and unique to the body concerned, as opposed to someone else's idea of good technique to which you have forced your body to conform. Which behavior is likely to lead to your optimum performance?

Tap the Emotions

The senses are one aspect of self-awareness. Another aspect is emotions, which have particular relevance to interpersonal problems at work or elsewhere.

Questions such as the following will be used:

- What do you feel when you are summoned unexpectedly to the boss's office?
- What emotions are you left with following the recent round of layoffs?
- What do you think you are afraid of?
- Where in your body do you experience tension?
- In what ways do you inhibit your potential?
- What is the predominant feeling you have when you know that you have done a good job?

- Can you give me a rating on a scale of one to ten for your level of confidence in your ability to give a good presentation this afternoon?

Self-awareness also needs to be brought to bear on our thoughts and attitudes in the moment, and on those to which we normally have less conscious access. Each of us brings with us, sometimes from our childhood, long-standing beliefs and opinions that will color our perceptions and our relationships with others. If we fail to acknowledge their existence and to compensate for their effects, our sense of reality will be distorted by them.

Assess the Attitudes

The Interconnectedness of Body and Mind

Most thoughts carry an emotion with them; all emotions are reflected in the body; body sensations often trigger thoughts. It follows, therefore, that concerns, blockages, and inhibitions can be approached through the mind, the body, or the emotions, and a clearing of one often tends to free the others. Persistent stress, for example, may be reduced by identifying body tensions; by evoking awareness of the feelings that fuel overwork; by uncovering mental attitudes like perfectionism. It may be necessary to work on all three separately. Here I remind you of Timothy Gallwey's theme that the player of the Inner Game improves performance by seeking to remove or reduce the inner obstacles to outer performance.

It is time for a word of caution. A coach may become aware of probing deeper into a coachee's hidden drives and motives than anticipated. That is the nature of coaching: it addresses causes, not merely symptoms. Coaching may be more demanding than papering over the interpersonal cracks in the office with directives, but it is also more rewarding in terms of results. However, if you are inadequately trained in coaching or faint-hearted, stay out of it! If you suspect that a staff relationship problem has deep-seated origins, then it is better to bring in a professional with the necessary skills. The boundary between coaching and counseling is only that

Limit the Depth

coaching is mainly *proactive* and counseling is generally *reactive*.

REALITY QUESTIONS

It is in this reality phase of coaching that questions should most often be initiated by the interrogatives *what, when, where, who,* and *how much. How* and *why* should be used sparingly or when no other phrase will suffice. Coaches will need to be especially alert, listening and watching to pick up all the clues that indicate the direction of questioning to be followed. It must be stressed here that it is the *coachee* whose awareness is being raised. The coach often does not need to know the whole history of a situation, but needs merely to be certain that the coachee is clear about it. This is, therefore, not as time-consuming as it would be were the coach to need all the facts in order to provide the best answer.

One reality question that nearly always contributes value is, "What action have you taken on this so far?" followed by, "What were the effects of that action?" This emphasizes the value of action, and the difference between actions and thinking about problems. Often people spend much time thinking about problems, but only when they are asked what they have done about them, do they realize that they have taken no action at all.

Early Resolutions

If the issue is one that requires a solution, it is surprising how often the thorough investigation of reality turns up the answer before one even enters the third and fourth stages of coaching. Obvious courses of action that emerge in the reality or, even on occasion, the goal stage are often accompanied by a "Eureka!" cry of recognition and an extra impulse to complete the task. The value of this is such that coaches should be willing to dwell sufficiently long in goals and reality and resist the temptation to rush on into options prematurely. To prevent us from doing that, let's revisit the coaching session that Mike is giving Joe.

Mike:	So much for your goals, Joe; let's have a look at things as they stand now. How much do you weigh?
Joe:	225 pounds in my clothes.
Mike:	When did you last weigh yourself?
Joe:	Last week sometime.
Mike:	Next door in the bathroom is a scale. Would you hop on it now?
Joe:	...Oh darn! I'm 235 pounds.
Mike:	Do you eat too much?
Joe:	Yes, I'm a chocoholic and I do like rich food.
Mike:	Have you been eating a lot recently?
Joe:	More than usual. I seem to eat when I'm worried.
Mike:	What are you worried about now?
Joe:	My health, middle age, and I feel insecure about my job.
Mike:	What bothers you most?
Joe:	My health, I suppose, because I'm convinced that if I could get a handle on that, my state of mind—and, therefore, my work—would improve.
Mike:	OK, let's stay with that for today, but in another session we could look specifically at your state of mind or your work. What do you eat too much of?
Joe:	Potato chips and desserts.
Mike:	At every meal?
Joe:	Most days both, at least once.
Mike:	At home or when you're out? At lunch or in the evenings?
Joe:	In the evenings at home, and when we eat out, at least two evenings a week.
Mike:	With friends or with your wife?
Joe:	Mainly when it's just the two of us.
Mike:	Does your wife like to eat a lot, too?

Joe: Not really, but she knows ... along with it.

Mike: So you like sweets and ch... you are worried, and do t... evenings and with the fa... drinking?

Joe: I sometimes have several b... and I usually have at least t... in the evening.

Mike: Exactly how many beers hav... last seven days?

Joe: Let me see...about 12.

Mike: And the week before?

Joe: About the same, if I'm honest.

Mike: Shall we look at exercise now?

Joe: OK. I have started running, at least.

Mike: How often do you run and for how long?

Joe: I run about fifteen minutes maybe twice a week.

Mike: When did you run this week?

Joe: I didn't, I just felt too miserable.

Mike: The week before?

Joe: Once on Sunday morning. I was going to run again, but my calves still hurt.

Mike: Does the discomfort of running put you off?

Joe: Yes. Ankles, calves, thighs, heaving breath—I hate it!

Mike: Do you do any other exercising—walking, bicycling, even running upstairs instead of taking the elevator?

Joe: No, but I do take an occasional sauna.

Mike: Do you like that and do you think it helps?

Joe: It helps relieve my guilt and it's not too strenuous.

Joe is now more honest with himself about the reality of his overindulgence in food and drink and of how minimal his exercise is. Joe's wishful thinking, or self-delusion, is now grounded in reality. What's even more important, he knows exactly where he is starting.

Mike then takes Joe back to review Joe's goal of 210 pounds, which is perhaps unrealistic because he actually weighs 235 pounds. However, Joe is so disgusted with the reality of his weight that he does not wish to alter the 210-pound target, even though this now requires an average reduction of more than three pounds a month. Mike still considers it to be realistic.

Fortunately, Mike offers to coach Joe on his running to try to reduce the discomfort he experiences, so this will give us the opportunity to hear an example of coaching a physical skill. Mike and Joe set out on a short run together, having agreed on a goal to find a comfortable running style, pace, and mental activity.

Mike: OK, let's find an initial speed that feels relatively comfortable…. What are you noticing in your body?

Joe: My calves feel stiff.

Mike: Just place all your attention on your calves and tell me exactly how they feel.

Joe: I feel a tightness down the back of them.

Mike: When do you feel it? All the time in both calves, or what?

Joe: No, just when I push off, and it's more in my right calf than in my left one.

Mike: Give your right calf a tightness rating on a scale of one to ten, with ten being as tight as you can imagine.

Joe: Actually it's less now, but it's about a five and the left leg is a three.

Mike: What is it now?

Joe: It's down to a three.

Mike: Keep monitoring it and tell me when it reaches two.

Joe:	Both calves are now a two or even less. They feel great, but I notice my arms hurt as I swing them.
Mike:	OK, just pay attention to the pain in your arms and tell me more about it.
Joe:	Hey, as soon as I started to pay attention to my arms, I felt them relax, and I notice that I'm now holding them in a lower position.
Mike:	Is that more comfortable, then?
Joe:	Yes, it certainly is.
Mike:	It actually looks more fluid as well.
Joe:	Yes, I really feel I'm moving quite well. Normally by this point my breath is heaving, but I notice that I'm breathing quite rhythmically.
Mike:	Just follow your breathing for a while. Don't try to breathe differently, but notice the in-breath and the outbreath as it happens each time.
Joe:	It's slowing down even more. I'll become a runner yet!
Mike:	What is the quality you would most like to find in your running?
Joe:	You mentioned it and I'm beginning to feel it flowing.
Mike:	OK, just rate how much you're flowing on a one-to-ten scale.
Joe:	Well, it was about a four, but it's already a six.
Mike:	Where in your body do you take your reading from?
Joe:	My shoulders, strangely enough.
Mike:	What is it now?
Joe:	It's an eight! I feel great!
Mike:	Yes, and we're back at base three minutes faster than you thought you could do it.
Joe:	That's amazing! I feel I could do another fifteen minutes, no sweat.

Mike: You will before long. Well done! You see how focusing the attention internally clears up problem areas, leads to relaxation, and is so interesting that boredom is eliminated. It turns a chore into a pleasure.

Joe: You never even told me how to run more efficiently, but I seem to have found that flow for myself. That makes me feel good, and opens up possibilities in other areas, too.

When in coaching purely to learn or to develop a physical skill on the field or in other areas of life, the process we use, repeated in different forms, of course, is complete at the end of this phase. The performance improvement takes place through the application of awareness during this reality phase, as it did for Joe. However, to improve Joe's overall health and well-being, and to further most business issues, which require planning, investigation, reviewing, and the like, there are two additional phases.

What Options Do You Have? 10

*T*he purpose of the *options* stage is not to find the "right" answer but to create and list as many alternative courses of action as possible. The *quantity* of options is more important here than the quality and feasibility of each one. It is from this broad base of creative possibilities that specific action steps will be selected. If preferences, censorship, ridicule, obstacles, or the need for completeness are expressed during the collection process, potentially valuable contributions will be missed and the choices will be limited.

MAXIMIZING CHOICES

The coach will do all he can to draw these options from the coachee or from the team he is coaching or managing. To do this he needs to create an environment in which participants will feel safe enough to volunteer their thoughts and ideas without inhibition or fear of judgment from the coach or others. All contributions, however apparently silly, need to be written down, usually by the coach, in case they contain a germ of an idea which may leap into significance in the light of later suggestions.

Negative Assumptions

Among the most restricting factors to our generation of creative solutions to business and other issues are the implicit assumptions we carry, many of which we are barely conscious. For example:

- It can't be done.
- It can't be done like that.
- They would never agree to that.
- It's bound to cost too much.
- We can't afford the time.
- The competition must have thought of that.

There are many more assumptions. Note that all of them contain a negative or a dismissal. A good coach would invite his coachees to ask themselves, "What if...?" For example:

- *What if* you had a large enough budget?
- *What if* you had more staff?
- *What if* you knew the answer? What would it be?
- *What if* that obstacle did not exist? What would you do then?

By this process, which temporarily sidesteps the censorship of the rational mind, more creative thought is unleashed and perhaps the obstacle is found to be less formidable than it had always seemed. Perhaps another team member might know a way around that particular obstacle, so the impossible is made possible by the combined contributions of more than one person.

The Nine-Dot Exercise

In our training courses for coaches, we use the well-known nine-dot exercise to illustrate graphically the self-limiting assumptions we all tend to make. For those unfamiliar with the exercise, or who have done it but may not remember the answer, here it is. The answers are at the end of the book.

Options

Nine-Dot Exercise

Can you join the nine dots, using four straight lines, without your writing implement leaving the page and without going over a line twice?

You may have remembered or realized that the assumption that has to be eliminated is the one that says, "You have to stay within the square." However, don't become too smug. Can you do it again with the same rules but using three lines or less? What assumptions are you limiting yourself with now?

No one said you had to draw your line through the middle of the dots, but I'll bet you assumed that. What about two lines, or even one?

No one said you could not tear the page out and roll it into a cone, tear it into three strips, or fold it like an accordion, but I bet you made one or more of those assumptions. Breaking out of these self-limiting assumptions frees us to solve old problems in new ways. The key is to identify the false assumption; the resolution is then much more easy to find.

Making the Choice

Benefits and Costs

Once a comprehensive list has been generated, the *will* phase of coaching may just be a simple matter of selecting the best of the bunch. However, in more complex issues, as so many in business are, it may be necessary to reexamine the list by noting the benefits and costs of each of the courses of action. This should again be done by coaching, and it is here that some blend of two or more ideas may emerge as the optimum.

Input From the Coach

What does the coach do if he has particular knowledge, skill, or experience in the matter in question and the coachee has not come up with what is, to the coach, the obvious solution? At what stage should the coach offer his expertise? Clearly, when he recognizes that the coachee has exhausted his possibilities. But how can he provide his input and still not undermine the sense of total ownership of the coachee? Quite simply by saying, "I have another couple of possible options. Would you like to have them?" Very few coachees will ever say no, but they might ask the coach to wait while they complete a particular train of thought. Any suggestions provided by the coach should only be accorded the same importance as all the other options.

Mapping the Options

In the listing of options, the subconscious hierarchy— which lists the more important things first—can be avoided by writing the options down randomly like the way someone solves a crossword puzzle.

Let's see how Mike, who happens to be a fitness buff himself, tackles the options issue with Joe, who clearly expects some prescription from the expert for his lack of fitness.

Mike: So what are all the different things you could do, Joe, to get yourself leaner and fitter?

Joe: I could run more often, or farther, or faster.

Mike: What else?

Joe: I could cut down on my eating and drinking.

Mike: What else?

Joe: I could eat fewer fatty foods.

Mike: What other forms of exercise could you do?

Joe: Oh well, I suppose I could go to the gym.

Mike: Anything else?

Joe: I could swim or even take up racquetball, which is something I've thought about at times. Or I could play golf.

Mike: Is there anything else you could do that requires no investment, no equipment, no clubs to join, just within your daily life?

Joe: I can't think of anything. I couldn't ride a bike, because I don't own one, and I'm not going to buy one for that!

Mike: What if you did have one?

Joe: I could ride it to work—and to the bar! I could actually walk to work and run up the stairs rather than take the elevator to the fourth floor.

Mike: Yes, you could. Is that it?

Joe: That's enough, isn't it?

Mike: Would you like one more option to consider?

Joe: Sure, if you have one.

Mike: How about weights and an exercise regimen at home?

Joe: Yes, that's possible, too.

Joe and Mike then examine the list and consider the advantages and disadvantages of these options. Golf is time-consuming. Racquetball is a much quicker and more strenuous form of exercise, but it takes a little time to learn to get the best out of it, and it requires a partner. The nearest swimming pool is five miles away, but swimming is injury-free. Together Joe and Mike explore the practicalities of certain diets and of being able to avoid alcohol in the business environment.

In case you are thinking that this example of coaching is a little removed from the business context, consider the following statement made by Sir Michael Edwardes in an interview with David Hemery from his book, *Sporting Excellence:*

> I am always very hesitant about bringing an unfit, overweight person onto a team; it suggests a lack of discipline. I am sixty and play squash three times a week and tennis once. I'm not overweight. My energy is greater than it was at fifty. I'm sure I'm fitter than my opposition and I think that is material. I wouldn't want anyone on my team who wasn't physically fit.

Joe is now aware of all the options and is pretty clear about their various pros and cons. Decision time has arrived.

What Will You Do? 11

The purpose of this final phase of the coaching sequence is to convert a discussion into a decision. It is the construction of an action plan to meet a requirement that has been clearly specified, on ground that has been thoroughly surveyed, and using the widest possible choice of building materials.

The following set of will questions are applicable to the majority of coaching situations. Of course, the coach will add subsets of questions to clarify each of these points, but the principle questions form an effective backbone for this phase.

The demands of an upper-level manager are often met with quiet resignation, resistance, or resentment, however diplomatically they are expressed. A coach, on the other hand, can bring a surprising degree of toughness into this phase of his questioning without causing any bad feelings, because he is not imposing his own will but activating the will of the coachee. The coachee always maintains choice and ownership, even if his decision is to take no action, and therefore he will not feel oppressed by hard questions. He might even be amused by the recognition of his own ambivalence. If he does feel pushed, it suggests that the coach is unconsciously revealing that he thinks the coachee *should* take a particular action.

Now let's look at the value, the objective, and the best way to ask each of these questions.

What Are You Going to Do?

This question is quite distinct from, "What could you do?" or "Which are you thinking of doing?" or "Which of these do you prefer?" None of these implies a firm decision. Once the coach has asked this question in a clear, firm voice, indicating that it is decision time, he may follow it up with a question like, "Which of these alternatives are you going to act on?" In most coaching issues, the action plan will incorporate more than one of the options or combine parts of the options.

The options have been only loosely defined. Now is time for the coach to ask questions to clarify the details of the chosen options. By far the most important of these will be the following:

When Are You Going to Do It?

This is the toughest of all the questions. We all have big ideas of what we would like to do or are going to do, but it is only when we create a time frame that the idea takes on a sense of reality. And an answer such as, "sometime next year" is insufficient. If something is going to happen, the timing needs to be highly specific.

If a single action is required, the answer sought might be, "At 10:00 A.M. next Tuesday, the 12th." Often both a starting time and date and a finishing date will be required. If the action to be followed is a repetitive one, then the intervals need to be specified: "We will meet at 9:00 A.M. on the first Wednesday of every month." It is up to the coach to nail the coachee down to exact times. The coachee may wriggle, but a good coach will not let him off the hook.

Will This Action Meet Your Goal?

Now that we have an action and a time frame, it is important, before we proceed any further, to check that this is leading in the direction of both the goal of the session and the long-term goal. Without checking back, the coachee may find that he has wandered a long way off track. If this has happened, it is important not to rush to change the action, but to check if, in fact, it is the goal that needs to be modified in the light of what has come up since it was defined.

What Obstacles Might You Meet Along the Way?

It is important to prepare for circumstances that could arise and inhibit completion of the action. Disruptive external scenarios might be looming, but internal ones could also be occuring, such as the faintheartedness of the coachee. Some people experience a shrinking commitment and just can't wait for an obstacle to appear and provide them with an excuse for not completing the goal. This can be prevented by using the coaching process.

Who Needs to Know?

Frequently in business, plans are changed and the people who should be promptly informed hear of the altered plans much later and secondhand, something that is very bad for staff relations. The coach needs to satisfy himself that all the appropriate people are listed and that a plan is made for them to be informed.

What support do you need? This is possibly related to the previous question, but support can come in many different forms. It could mean arranging to bring in outside people, skills, or resources, or it could be as simple as informing a colleague of your intention and asking her to remind you or keep you on target. Merely sharing your intended action with another human being often has the effect of ensuring that you follow through with it.

How and When Are You Going to Get That Support?

It is no good to want some support but to fail to take the steps necessary to get it. Here the coach needs to persist until the coachee's actions are clear and certain.

What Other Considerations Do You Have?

This is a necessary, catchall question so that the coachee cannot claim that the coach omitted something. It is the coachee's responsibility to ensure that nothing is left out.

Rate the Degree of Certainty You Have That You'll Carry Out the Agreed Actions

This is not rating on a one-to-ten scale the certainty that the outcome will actually happen. It is a rating of the coachee's intention to carry out her part of the job. Completion of the task may depend on the agreement or the actions of others, and that cannot be rated.

If you have rated yourself at less than eight, how can you reduce the size of the task or lengthen the time-scale such that it would enable you to raise the rating to eight or above?

If your rating is still below eight, cross out the action step, as you are unlikely to take it. This is not to sabotage completion, as it might appear, but it is our experience that those who rate at less than eight seldom follow through. However, when faced with having to admit failure, the coachee may all of a sudden find the necessary motivation.

Most of us are familiar with the items that keep recurring on our job lists, be it at work or just odd jobs around the home. Our list becomes so crumpled and scribbled on that eventually we rewrite it, and those same few items keep getting carried over. In time we begin to feel appropriately guilty but still nothing happens. "How is it that I never complete the list?" we moan to ourselves. Our ongoing job list is evidence of our failure. Well, why feel bad about it? If you are not going to do something, cross it off your list. And if you want to be a success from now on, don't put anything on your list that you do not intend to do!

CONCLUDING THE COACHING CYCLE

At this point the coaching cycle is complete, but it is up to the coach to hand to the coachee a clear and accurate written record of the action steps agreed on and the coachee's answers to all the will questions. He should have the coachee read it and confirm that it is an accurate record, that it constitutes his plan, that he fully understands it, and that he intends to carry it out. This is when I, as coach, usually offer myself as further support and reassure the coachee of my accessibility should he need me. Sometimes I offer to initiate the contact myself after a suitable interval just to see how things are going. This helps the coachee realize that he is important. I want the coachee to leave the session feeling good about himself and about his chances of getting the job done. If he does, then the task will be accomplished. Let's look at how Mike handles this final and important will phase with Joe.

Mike:	Well, Joe, we have a list here; let me remind you.

       Running more often, farther, or faster
       Eating and drinking less and more healthily
       Visiting a gym
       Swimming
       Racquetball
       Golf
       Cycling
       Walking
       Running upstairs
       Lifting weights and/or exercising at home

	Which of these are you going to do?
Joe:	I am definitely going to continue running, with a minimum of three times a week for twenty minutes.
Mike:	When are you going to start that?
Joe:	Next week, with the first run on Tuesday.
Mike:	Which day and what time each day are you going to run?

Joe: Usually Tuesday and Thursday, immediately after I get home from work, and on Sunday mornings. On Sundays I'll do half an hour.

Mike: Are you going to do anything else?

Joe: Yes, I'm going to cut out chips and chocolate altogether.

Mike: What about alcohol?

Joe: I was hoping you wouldn't ask that one directly! But yes, no more wine and only one light beer a day.

Mike: Is that realistic? Can you stick to one light beer if you are with friends?

Joe: Probably not.

Mike: I have a suggestion.

Joe: What?

Mike: Five light beers a week. If you overdo it one day, you just hold off the next one or two to make good.

Joe: Sounds good—much easier to stick to but with the same result.

Mike: When do you start?

Joe: Sunday.

Mike: Any other exercise?

Joe: I'll arrange for a couple of racquetball lessons to see if I like it and when I can get started.

Mike: When?

Joe: I knew you were going to ask that! I'll call the pro today and have my first lesson next week.

Mike: And the next lesson?

Joe: The following week.

Mike: Anything else?

Joe: Well, I'm certainly not going to start bicycling to work in the winter. I'll put that on the shelf for reconsideration on April 1.

Mike: I'll remind you (taking out his diary), and I'm not fooling either!

Joe:	Perhaps I could do a few exercises at home in the meantime.
Mike:	What exercises, and how often?
Joe:	You're the expert; you tell me.
Mike:	We'll come back to that one. Is that it?
Joe:	That should be more than enough to meet my goal.
Mike:	I agree, but is it realistic?
Joe:	I think so.
Mike:	Now, what obstacles can you foresee?
Joe:	Christmas for the food and drink, and extreme weather for the running. That's all. Oh, and my natural laziness.
Mike:	How will you cope with those obstacles?
Joe:	Give myself an extra couple of light beers that week and a bag of chips! I go on vacation the week after Christmas and I'll do two extra runs.
Mike:	What if there's bad frost or snow then or at any other time?
Joe:	I'll replace the running with either racquetball or a swim. I know what you're going to ask. Forty minutes of racquetball or twenty lengths of the pool.
Mike:	What about this laziness of yours, which we all have?
Joe:	I need a prod every now and then.
Mike:	Just what I was coming to. What support do you need and from whom?
Joe:	From my wife to help me avoid the food and to prompt me to run. I'll speak to her about all this tonight.
Mike:	Any other support you'll need?
Joe:	From you, a phone call every couple of weeks would help, and I'd like you to show me a couple of good exercises I can do at home. I don't want to buy weights and all that.

Mike: Sure, sit-ups like this don't require someone to hold your feet and are just as good for the stomach muscles. Start with ten and build up your repeats. Squats like this, and push-ups would help. Again, groups of repetitions are better than forcing. About ten minutes each day would be great.

Joe: OK, I'll do them each morning when I get up, and if I miss one morning, I've got a second chance in the evening. If I miss a whole day, I'll do two sets the following day.

Mike: When are you going to start this?

Joe: How about tomorrow morning?

Mike: You've been surprisingly willing to set yourself a fairly ambitious program, given your past history. How would you rate your chances of sticking to it for the next three months on a one-to-ten scale?

Joe: That's a tough one—seven, I guess.

Mike: Is there some part of this you could drop or reduce so you could give yourself a higher rating?

Joe: I think it's just too much, and I'm doubtful about the racquetball because I won't be able to do that on my own, when I want, and at short notice. If I drop that, I'll give myself a nine.

Mike: Good. One final check, is this regimen meeting your goal?

Joe: I've altered its emphasis, but I think it exceeds my goal and I'm very confident I'll succeed.

Not all coaching sessions are as straightforward as this one, and coachees can offer more resistance and complications, but this is fairly typical and it serves to illustrate the majority of the coaching principles.

And, as I have said before, most coaching sessions will be less formal and less structured than this one. Most take place in a way that might not even be recognized by the uninitiated as coaching. They would simply think that someone was being particularly helpful and considerate of the other person, and was obviously a good listener. Whether structured or informal, the fundamental principles of raising awareness and building responsibility within the performer remain the keys to good coaching.

What Is Performance? **12**

" *T*he execution of the functions required of one"
is how my dictionary defines performance, but
that sounds a lot like doing the minimum necessary to
get by. That is not performance in my book; it is not what
I refer to in *Coaching for Performance*.

Real performance is going *beyond* what is expected; it
is setting one's own highest standards, invariably standards that surpass what others demand or expect. It is an
expression of one's potential. This comes closer to the
second meaning of performance as defined by my dictionary: "a deed, a feat, a public exhibition of skill." That
is what I try to bring out in those that I coach.

By definition, the full expression of one's potential
demands taking total responsibility or ownership. If it
did not, it would not be one's potential; it would be
partly someone else's. Coaching is, therefore, the essential management style or tool for optimizing people's
potential and performance. Commanding, demanding,
instructing, or persuading with threats that are overt or

covert, cannot produce sustainable optimum performance, even though all may get the job done.

The question a leader or a manager has to ask herself is how well she wants the job done or how good a performance she seeks. Does she even know what a really good performance would look like? Coaching can lead to performance beyond the expectations of the coach or manager, and beyond the dreams of the performer.

In sports, where success and failure are so clearly defined, the rules are simple, the time span is short, and physical or mental discomfort can determine the outcome, self-motivation is not hard to evoke. The news media would have us believe that fame and fortune are the dream of every sports performer. For some, perhaps, but the majority of athletes are shooting for less-tangible goals like identity, self-esteem, excellence, and peak experience—uniquely personal rewards experienced only by the performer.

Success in business, by comparison, is less glamorous, and slower to come. Quality of life in the workplace, by virtue of the hours and years spent there, takes on a far greater importance. Few chief executives achieve any degree of public recognition, and those that do are likely to be more infamous than famous. On the other hand, business offers countless opportunities, both large and small, for personal achievement of goals that can be individually chosen to provide optimal personal growth. Unfortunately, few people view their workplace as a university for self-development or their responsibilities as challenges. It is hardly surprising, therefore, that their performance lacks sparkle.

THE JOHNSONVILLE SAUSAGE SAGA

Let me tell you the story of Johnsonville Sausage. That was the name of a family-owned sausage-making business in Wisconsin, which in 1980 was under the stewardship of Ralph Stayer. Stayer wrote about his company in the November/December 1990 issue of the *Harvard Business Review* under the title "How I Learned to Let My Workers Lead."

Growth, sales, and profits were good at Johnsonville Sausage, giving all the indications of a successful business, but... "What worried me more than the competition, however, was the gap between potential and performance," wrote Stayer. "No one was deliberately wasting money, time, and materials; it was just that people took no responsibility for their work. They showed up in the morning, did half-heartedly what they were told to do, and then went home."

The situation that Stayer describes is common, but he clearly recognized the vital role responsibility plays in bringing performance up to potential. On his own admission, Stayer then "went from authoritarian control to authoritarian abdication." He forced responsibility on his management team and expected them to guess what he wanted. It did not work. "The early 1980s taught me that I couldn't give responsibility. People had to expect it, want it, even demand it.... To bring people to that...I had to learn to be a better coach."

He changed his approach. The sausage makers, instead of the top management, started tasting the sausages and took charge of quality control and of making improvements to the product and its packaging. Next, the workers raised the issue of poor-performing colleagues.

> We offered to help them set performance standards and to coach them in confronting poor performers, but we insisted that since they were the production performance experts it was up to them to deal with the situation. I bit my tongue time and time again, but they took on the responsibility for dealing with performance problems and actually fired individuals who wouldn't perform up to the standards of their teams.

Before long the Johnsonville work force was responsible for the vast majority of functions. Terms like "employee" and "subordinate" were dropped in favor of "members" of the organization, and managers became known as "coordinators" or "coaches." This change in language set the tone of the renewed organization, in which promotion came from ability as a teacher, coach, and facilitator, rather than from managing or problem-solving in the traditional sense.

Stayer noticed that the work force

> wanted to see if I practiced what I preached. From the outset I did simple things to demonstrate my sincerity. I made a sign for my desk that said, "the question is the answer," and when people came in to me with questions, I asked myself if they were questions I should answer. Invariably they weren't. Invariably people were asking me to make decisions for them. Instead of giving answers, I turned the tables and asked the questions myself, trying to make them repossess their own problems.

As time went on the "members" were empowered to make strategic decisions, and did so successfully, and Stayer even began to see himself as a consultant to his own company.

> When I began this process of change ten years ago, I looked forward to the time when it would be all over and I could get back to my real job. But I've learned that *change* is the real job of every effective business leader because change is about the present and the future, not about the past. There is no end to change. Yet another thing I've learned is that the cause of excitement at Johnsonville Sausage is not change itself but the process used in producing change. Learning and responsibility are invigorating, and aspirations make our hearts beat.
>
> Getting better performance from any group or individual, yourself included, means permanent change in the way you think and run your business. Change of this kind is not a single transaction but a journey, and the journey has a specific starting point *[reality]* and a clear destination *[goal]*.
>
> So to make the changes that will lead to great performance, I recommend focusing on goals, expectations, contexts, actions, and learning.

Stayer clearly practices what he preaches. The work force is responding with performance that is exceptional, and no doubt learning and enjoyment are very high, too, at Johnsonville Sausage. It takes courage to initiate such radical changes in any organization, but any business leader who seeks to be assured of real performance, and perhaps survival in the uncertain future, will do well to consider big changes. But where do they start?

Coaching for performance improvement in self, in others, and in teams is simple and straightforward, provided its underlying principles are fully embraced, and the adoption of a coaching management style is where change begins. One caution, however. Managers, even those who use coaching widely, may fail if they focus exclusively on performance improvement. Performance, learning, and enjoyment are inextricably intertwined. All three are enhanced by high awareness levels, a fundamental objective of coaching, but it is possible to focus primarily on the development of one of them quite successfully, though only for a while. When one of the three is neglected, sooner or later the other two will suffer. For example, performance cannot be sustained where there is no learning or where there is no enjoyment. Many professional sports performers have experienced periods of losing the enjoyment of their sport. Likewise, the enjoyment of basking on a beach may fade after a day or three and as we begin to seek challenges to our performance with tennis or new skills to learn like scuba diving. Schools of learning that do not offer the challenges of the performing arts or sports and that frown on enjoyment are unable to maintain the high standards of learning they so urgently and exclusively seek. The very definition of performance, for coaching purposes, should include learning and enjoyment, too.

Assessment and Application **13**

*S*o far we have considered coaching as a tool for addressing existing issues of planning, problem-solving, reviewing, skill development, and so forth. In this chapter I am going to demonstrate how coaching can be applied to any developmental or performance-improvement requirements.

THE AWARENESS LIST

In "business speak" we hear a lot about identifying strengths and weaknesses of personnel, processes, and products. We can list the strengths and weaknesses of each of these and, indeed, of ourselves. We can list other things, too, such as the qualities required of a prospective employee, those behaviors we would like to foster in a work team, or those we would like to develop in ourselves. We can list the functions of our organization, a department, or an individual. We can list technical skills, interpersonal skills, or manual skills required. Breaking things down into more detail like this is one level of awareness-raising.

We can use this list to take this awareness-raising a step further if we then rate these strengths, weaknesses, qualities, functions, or skills on our now-familiar one-to-ten scale, either in terms of what we would like them to be, or what we think they are now.

SELF-ASSESSMENT

In business, much importance is accorded to assessing others—peers, subordinates, or even bosses. But, in my opinion, self-assessment is the most productive form of assessment. Ratings on skills and qualities given by and to others is best regarded as feedback—valuable input on which we can choose to act—rather than as a judgment or the truth, which may have a disempowering impact on us. A video, on the other hand, shows the reality of what happened in a situation, but should be used to inform a person rather than to criticize them. Self-assessment bypasses the negative effects of criticism and places responsibility where it needs to be to prompt effective action and self-improvement. Let me give an example.

Qualities

The qualities and skills I need to do my job well are listed below in random order of importance. In the first column opposite each skill I wrote how I rate myself, and in the second column I wrote the rating I could reasonably hope to achieve.

	At Present	Target
Communicative	8	9
Empathetic	6	9
Patient	7	9
Computer literate	4	7
Administratively capable	6	8
Enthusiastic	8	8
Alert and observant	8	9
Bookkeeping competency	5	7

By doing this I have raised my self-awareness, but in terms of the coaching process, I have done more than that. The first column represents the reality and the second column represents a realistic, specific, measurable, positively stated, challenging goal. All I need to do is select which one I want to work on, put it in a time frame, and I will have completed the first two stages of a simple self-coaching process.

I need to take some time to list all the options I have for developing my chosen skill or quality. If I have selected a quality, I might want to list the positive behaviors associated with people who have an abundance of that quality. The reason for this is that action taken will usually be in the form of new behaviors, rather than new qualities, which take longer to develop. In time it is the success of these new behaviors that will enable me to rate myself higher in terms achieving of the underlying qualities.

Finally, I will ask myself the will questions and present myself with an action plan.

Team Assessment

Variations of this exercise can be used on oneself, on individuals, and with teams. It is particularly interesting to have team members list desirable team qualities and then rate their team on each. The disparity between the figures offers opportunities to discuss the different criteria by which people assess and the different opinions that various members have of the same team.

For example, members of a five-person team were each asked to list the four most important team qualities. Their lists turned out as follows:

Joe	Mike	Susan	Valerie	David
Humor	Trust	Support	Cooperation	Tolerance
Patience	Courage	Flexibility	Trust	Cohesion
Support	Cooperation	Enthusiasm	Compatibility	Trust
Friendship	Adaptability	Unselfishness	Support	Commitment

A merged list was formed from these lists. Cooperation and cohesion were considered to be the same, as were adaptability and flexibility. Each of the team members was asked to rate the team on each quality. They were asked to do this individually on paper before the figures were brought to the flip chart. No member's figures were influenced by the figures of the others. The results were as follows:

	Joe	Mike	Susan	Valerie	David	Average
Support	7	8	4	6	6	6.2
Cooperation	8	7	8	6	9	7.6
Trust	7	5	5	7	5	5.8
Adaptability	9	7	8	9	6	7.8
Patience	7	8	4	6	8	6.6
Friendship	9	9	7	5	4	6.8
Commitment	8	8	9	8	8	8.2
Courage	5	6	7	7	8	6.6
Humor	8	6	3	4	5	5.2
Enthusiasm	7	7	8	6	7	7.0
Compatibility	6	6	6	7	6	6.2
Unselfishness	8	7	6	8	6	7.0
Tolerance	7	6	6	6	5	6.0

In this case they were not asked to add to the above ratings (a highly personal figure), their rating of how much of each of these qualities they personally contribute to the team. Nor were they asked to rate each other's contribution to the sum total of these qualities in the team. Ratings of this kind can open up huge discussions, disputes, love affairs, and several cans of worms. If I, however, were to work with a team that was going for gold or on whom my life depended, I would want to rate personal contributions.

What the above figures show is that trust is an issue that needs work, that Joe's brand of humor is not much appreciated, particularly by the women, that Susan feels defensive at times, and that David feels isolated. There is plenty of scope for individual coaching here, by a peer or by an outside facilitator, and for a team discussion of options and a team agreement of what actions they will take to raise the level of several of these qualities.

Reframing Weaknesses

Coaching to build qualities in teams or individuals is a way of positively framing weaknesses and is far more creative and likely to achieve success than attempting to exorcise the weakness. There are an infinite number of variations of the coaching exercises that can be devised from this basis model, and examples to suit all kinds of situations. Now it's your turn to try your hand at coaching skills.

The Development of a Team **14**

*W*e have begun to explore ways of coaching with a team to improve its performance, but we need to understand some of the dynamics of team development if we are to get the best out of our team. I use a simple three-stage model that is easy to understand and in which each stage is readily recognized in most teams. More complex and sophisticated models exist, but, in my experience, they are of less practical use.

For the purposes of this model, the number of team members can range from a handful to an entire nation. Teams of more than fifteen or twenty members are likely to be made up of subteams, but whether it is a first team or a sub-subsubteam, certain characteristics remain the same.

HIGH-PERFORMING TEAMS

The model I use blends well with the team-qualities exercise in the previous chapter. Using the views of those team members, for example, we could safely say that an effective, high-performing team would be well endowed with:

Support	Cooperation
Trust	Adaptability
Patience	Friendship
Commitment	Courage
Humor	Enthusiasm
Compatibility	Unselfishness

A team that could reasonably be rated at ten for each of these qualities would indeed be a high-performing team, and an exceptional one. So how can one get a team to perform this well? Some people would say it requires the right chemistry and a lot of luck. Others might not be so convinced that it would be such a great team, believing that some internal friction and competition generate good performance. They could believe that only because they have never seen a better team. Rare as they may be—both in business and in sports—such teams do exist.

Luck or Judgment?

While high-performing teams have, in the past, often come about by luck, some have been developed through the understanding and efforts of the team members and their leader. One such team was the English field-hockey team that won the gold medal at the 1988 Seoul Olympics. The coach who was largely responsible for their team development was David Whitaker, with whom I now work closely. Whitaker said of the team: "They became a harmonious, dynamic unit without negating the special individual talents that each player contributed."

Stages of Team Development

The first requirement of a team leader is to understand fully the stages through which a team will develop in order to encourage and accelerate the process. If we call the ideal team state the *cooperation* stage, how would we characterize the two stages through which it has to pass before it reaches the cooperation stage, if it ever does?

Inclusion

The first stage is called the *inclusion* stage, for it is here that people determine if they are, and if they feel they are, team members. Anxiety and introversion are common, but they may be disguised by compensatory opposite behavior in some people. Perhaps your family moved when you were a child and you suddenly found yourself plunged into a new school of strangers in the middle of the school year. You will recall the feelings well: feelings of separateness and the desperate need to find a friend, to feel included, to be like the others, and to be liked. Group members may not be very mentally productive in this phase, for their focus will be on their emotional needs and concerns.

If there is a designated group leader the members will look to him for acceptance and guidance. The tone and the example that the leader sets at this stage is important because it will quickly become the accepted norm of the group. For example, if the leader displays openness and honesty and discloses feelings or even a weakness of his own, others will tend to follow suit, and a good practice of relating will be established. It is a time of tentativeness, and a good leader will attempt to address and satisfy individual concerns so that the group as a whole can move forward. Fortunately, for many people this phase does not last long, but, for a few, it may take weeks or months to feel a part of the team. Those who had a childhood in which they developed a strong sense of personal security—and those who rise to leadership positions tend to be this type—would do well to be tolerant and supportive of those who were not so lucky.

Assertion

Once the majority of the group feels included, another dynamic emerges, that of individual *assertion*. It is a time of expressing power and of extending boundaries. Animals do it; they mark their territory, and woe to any opponent who dares enter. This is the phase in which the pecking order is established. The polite business phrase for it is the "establishment of roles and functions," but the words are often nicer than the actions. Competition within the team is hot, which may even lead to exceptional individual performances, sometimes at the expense of others. It is a phase in which people try out and discover their strengths, and the team may make up in productivity for what it lacks in cohesiveness.

This is an important and valuable development phase, but it can be tough for the leader. There will be challenges for the leadership position. Team members have to find out that they can disagree with the leader before they will be willing to agree. They need to exercise their will internally, in order to hone it for team application externally. A good group leader will offer—and encourage team members to take—responsibilities and thereby satisfy their assertion needs. It is important that the leader allows the challenges, but unfortunately, many leaders feel threatened when they are challenged. They hunker down and assert their own authority in order to control the process. It requires a balancing act.

Those who run training groups often experience this phase in which the leader's role is challenged. In a five-day group training session, the day on which this phase materializes is called the "kill the trainer" day. It generally begins toward the evening of the second day, but a good leader usually manages to be "resurrected" during the third day. If this phase coincides with the visit of an outside presenter, he may be given a very rough ride for little apparent reason. This is all a necessary, even healthy, part of group dynamics, but often, the interplays remain covert for the sake of appearances, and they therefore take longer to work themselves out.

A team in this phase can be quite productive, which may shield the recognition of yet greater potential. In fact, the majority of business or sports teams seldom advance beyond this phase, by and large because that phase is about as far as our whole Western industrial society has collectively reached. To go beyond this is therefore to go above the norm, but that is not as difficult to achieve as is generally thought—with coaching.

Cooperation

At the beginning of this chapter we examined some of the most positive characteristics prevalent in the *cooperation* phase of a team. I do not wish to imply that such a team would be all sweetness and light. In fact, a danger

Team Development Stage		Characteristics		Maslow's Hierarchy of Needs
Cooperation (performing)	Interdependent	Energy directed outward to common goals	Freedom	Self-actualized Self-realized
(norming)				
Assertion (storming)	Independent	Energy focused on internal competition	Greed	Self-esteem Esteem of others
Inclusion (forming)	Dependent	Energy turned inward within team members	Need	Belonging

of the cooperation stage is that an overemphasis on the group develops, which becomes too comfortable and which does not allow for any dissent. The most productive teams will be highly cooperative but will retain a degree of dynamic tension. The best team leaders preserve this sensitively.

The table shows, in parentheses, another set of labels for the same team-developmental sequence, and also some of the main distinguishing team characteristics. There are more.

For example, if a team is in the cooperation stage and one of its members has a bad day, the others will rally 'round and support the team member. If the group is in the assertion stage, the others may quietly celebrate the fall of a competitor. If it is in the inclusion stage, few will know or care.

On the other hand, if a team is in the cooperation stage and a team member has a personal triumph, the rest will join in the celebration. However, if the team is in the assertion stage, the rest may become jealous. If the team is in the inclusion stage, the others could feel threatened.

Maslow's Hierarchy of Needs

I also draw the parallel to Maslow's Hierarchy of Human Needs, with which many readers will be familiar. The primary *survival* and *safety* needs are largely collectively met in our "civilized" world, so the foremost needs that remain partially unfulfilled are the *belonging* needs. In today's world *self-esteem* and the *esteem* of others are often sought through successfully competing against others in business or in sports. Only when these needs are met is the self-actualizing individual freed from compelling ego needs and able to cooperate fully for the greater good of the whole.

A team of self-actualized individuals, if they could be found, would quickly attain the cooperation stage of development and produce outstanding performances as a result. A team comprising principally those seeking esteem would be far from cohesive, but stellar individual performances would not be uncommon. A team of individuals anxious to be liked and to belong would hardly perform at all.

Of course, the divisions between these three stages are permeable and overlapping, and the position and state of the team is subject to fluctuation when there is any turnover in team personnel.

Nevertheless, few readers will fail to recognize these stages and their characteristics from their own experiences at work or play. One macrocosmic example to challenge your mind is the suggestion that the whole of Western industrial society is in the latter days of the assertion stage, with a few early signs of cooperation showing through (i.e., the Live Aid and similar philanthropic concerts; the concern for the environment; and the integration of Europe). The collapse of the Soviet empire was the inevitable result of the attempt to coerce that society into the cooperation stage without allowing the organic progression through the previous stages. And the attempts to redraw the map in Eastern Europe and elsewhere is the manifestation of the temporary backslide into the inclusion issues. For some, even *survival* and *safety* are paramount.

So if we can accept the idea that development of this general nature is common among teams of all shapes and sizes, it follows that we can resist and thereby hinder team development, or we can encourage and accelerate team development. Because the members of a cooperative team will, by their very nature, be more aware and more self-responsible than most, it is obvious that coaching is a key skill of team development. How coaching is best applied with teams is addressed in the following chapter.

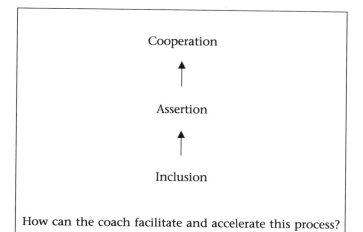

Cooperation

↑

Assertion

↑

Inclusion

How can the coach facilitate and accelerate this process?

Coaching Teams **15**

*I*t is most important for a manager to establish a "right" relationship with the team members under his charge from the moment he meets them. His behavior will be taken by the team members as the model for their behavior. They will tend to emulate him, even though initially they are likely to do so primarily as a means of gaining his approval while they are in the inclusion stage of team development.

Coaching by Example

If the team leader wishes to establish openness and honesty in the team, then he needs to be open and honest from the outset. If he wants the team members to trust him and each other, he must demonstrate trust and trustworthiness. If he sees a benefit in social contact outside work among the team, then he needs to participate in, and perhaps initiate, it himself.

Because the majority of individuals and teams still expect somewhat authoritarian leadership, they might be surprised, even confused, by a leader who begins on a very participative note. A few might even imagine him to be weak or unsure of himself. It is advisable for him to preempt this immediately by describing his intended management style and inviting questions about it.

The manager or team leader also needs to be clear about his willingness to invest his own time and energy in developing quality, long-term relationships and performances in his team, as opposed to the short-term goal of merely getting the job done . If the manager only pays lip service to team-building principles, he will get no more than he pays for. Dedication to team process pays off.

Coaching is the primary tool for both managing and developing teams. Peter Lenney, a general manager in Courtaulds Coatings, told *Management Today* (December, 1991) that "if you can't coach, you can't manage" became something of a corporate axiom. I agree wholeheartedly.

David Kenney, management development manager of Boots the Chemist, says that part of his mission is "to ensure that 100 percent of our managers behave as good coaches."

THE APPLICATION OF COACHING IN TEAMS

The team development model described in the previous chapter forms an excellent basis for the application of coaching in teams. If the manager or coach understands that teams perform at their best when they reach the cooperation stage, then he will use coaching with the team as a whole and with individual members to generate upward progress through the stages. For example, if the agreed goal is to lift the team into the cooperation stage and the reality is that it is now somewhere between the inclusion and the assertion stages, what options do we have and what will we do?

Options to Achieve Team Cooperation

The list of options that follows has been compiled from the responses to the question in the previous paragraph asked by participants in the team-building programs that I run.

1. Discuss and agree on a set of common goals for the team.

This should be done within the team, regardless of whether the organization has defined the team's goal. There is always room for modification and for deciding how it should be done. Each team member should be invited to contribute and to add any personal goals he or she has which might be embraced within the overall team goal.

2. Develop a set of ground rules or operating principles acceptable to all team members and to which all have contributed.

All should agree to abide by these rules even if individuals are not wholeheartedly behind all of the rules. If they want to have their wishes included, it is essential that they agree to respect others'. These ground rules should be monitored to ensure they are being adhered to and whether or not they need to be changed or updated. If all parties agree to these rules in sincerity and have good intentions, harsh recriminations should not be made for lapses in abiding by the rules unless they become frequent.

Many of the suggestions that follow could be included as ground rules, but I will list them separately here.

3. Set aside time on a regular basis, usually in conjunction with a scheduled task meeting, for group process work.

During this time ground rules are reviewed, appreciations and gripes are expressed, and personal sharing might be included so that openness and trust are built. Team members should be acknowledged as people, not just as cogs in a production machine. This period should not be allowed to be taken over by task talk.

4. Canvass team members' views about the desirability of arranging structured social time together.

If a regular event is planned, the preference of an individual not to attend because of prior commitments or the need for more family time must be respected. The person, however, needs to be prepared for some feeling of separateness as a consequence of his choice.

5. Put support systems in place to deal, in confidence if requested, with individual troubles or concerns as they arise.

If process meetings cannot be held frequently for geographical or other reasons, a buddy system might be instituted whereby each member of the team has another member as a buddy to whom he or she can talk if needed. This way minor issues can be resolved promptly and valuable process meeting time is not wasted.

6. Develop a common interest outside work.

Some teams have found that a group activity such as a sport or a common interest outside work that is shared by all can be very binding for the team. I recall one team who "adopted" a child in a developing country and, with a small monthly contribution each, paid for her schooling. They felt that she had contributed even more to their lives than they had to hers.

7. Learn a new skill together.

Similar to the previously mentioned option, but more task oriented, some teams have agreed to learn a new skill, like coaching, or to attend a work-related course together. This might even be in healthy competition with other regional teams, for example, in the same organization.

8. Practice the qualities exercise together.

Team relationships benefit greatly when team members practice appropriate variations among themselves of the qualities exercise explained in Chapter 13. This throws light on certain qualities, thereby helping to grow them. It also builds trust, understanding, and openness among team members remarkably quickly. It can be repeated in similar or different forms on a regular basis, for example, at every other process meeting.

9. Hold group discussions on individual and collective meaning and purpose as perceived by group members.

This is both broader and deeper than exploring goals. Meaning and purpose are what drive people, and a lack of them leads to lethargy, depression, and poor health. Throwing more light or awareness on something that is so pervasive will increase purposefulness and the quality of life at work and at home.

Each of these suggestions or options can be considered by the team using a coaching approach. They may be introduced or quietly facilitated by the team leader, but should be decided on by the team members themselves. The decision to adopt one or more of them must be made democratically, but it also must be specific and recorded in ways recommended in Chapter 11. Remember that the basis of coaching to improve team performance is not imposing but increasing individual and collective awareness and responsibility.

Overcoming Barriers to Coaching 16

W^e have looked at the context of coaching, its value, and its irrefutable logic. There is no mystique about coaching. It is not difficult to learn. However, it cannot be learned from a book, any more than driving a car or driving a golf ball can. Like all skills, it requires practice. If that practice is undertaken with commitment, and with awareness and responsibility, it does not take long to become proficient and relaxed in its use, and to benefit from its results.

A New Vision of People

For some people, coaching both demands and causes a fundamental change in the way they perceive themselves and others, such as colleagues, subordinates, or competitors. A coaching outlook regards all people as having the potential to be great in their chosen field, just as an acorn has the potential to become a towering oak tree. This is a far cry from the more common, but outmoded, perception of people as empty vessels of little worth until they are given outside input. That shift may take time or it may come as a revelation. However, even before it takes place, and while the underlying philosophy still seems foreign, it is possible to raise performance levels quite effectively by simply following the principles of good coaching prescribed in this book.

Nothing is smooth sailing, however, and you are liable to meet a few barriers along the way. There are external and internal barriers. In the coaching courses I provide for managers, I always ask them to list the barriers they think they might run into; then we explore ways of overcoming each of them. I draw the most common concerns from those lists and offer some challenging comments on each of them.

EXTERNAL BARRIERS

1. The company culture is against this kind of coaching approach.

A coaching philosophy is part of the new company culture that the enlightened people in your organization are trying to create. Others prefer the boring illusion of the security of the status quo. However, more and more organizations are coming to the conclusion that survival in the future may depend on change now, and that the status quo is actually the riskier alternative.

2. People are cynical toward any new approach.

Yes, people probably will be cynical, especially if communication within your organization has not been the best. It is important to tell people what you will do differently, and why.

3. People won't understand what I'm doing and won't trust me.

Same objections as above.

4. They'll know I've been to a course and will give me a few weeks to get back to "normal."

Same objections as above.

5. They'll think my new approach is just a new management gimmick.

Explain that it is not a gimmick but a necessity for improved performance and for improved staff relations. People will soon discover that it is no gimmick, unless that is how you yourself see it.

6. It takes too long—I would rarely have the time to coach.

It all depends how you measure your time. It is usually quicker to tell people what to do, but if they quickly forget and you have to tell them again...and again...and again, or if you have to keep looking over their shoulder, which takes longer?

Let me quote a user of coaching, Cameron Burness, a production-plant manager with ICI Pharmaceuticals.

> Everything I do is essentially performance-aimed. I use coaching as a means of getting my staff to a level where I can delegate work to them which I would otherwise have to do myself. I see the time I spend coaching very much as an investment, the dividend from which is the far greater time I save myself through delegation.

If there were a fire, I wouldn't hesitate to yell, "Get out of here!" but, unless I actively seek opportunities to grow my staff by coaching them, I will be stuck in the firefighting cycle.

7. They expect to be told.

If they have always been told in the past, then they will expect to be told. That is not the same thing as *preferring* to be told.

8. They want to be told—they don't want to take responsibility.

If people have never been given responsibility by their parents, at school, or at work, it will seem scary at first, like anything new. Underneath, the majority of us crave responsibility, in part because it provides us with a measure of self-worth. Those with very low self-worth have a hard time with responsibility. It is another cycle to get stuck in, but coaching is the best way I know to help people out of it. A few of the relevant coaching questions might be:

- What do you want from work, apart from money?
- What does responsibility mean to you?
- Do you feel a burden of responsibility right now?
- Is responsibility always a burden to you?
- What do you think some people like about responsibility?
- What else are you responsible for in your life?
- What are you afraid of?
- What could you do to overcome that?
- What are you willing to take responsibility for?
- Are you willing to try accepting more responsibility for a week?

Merely by answering these questions, people are beginning to take on responsibility—at least for their own answers and choices. If you, as their manager, won't help them take responsibility, who will? And are you satisfied with the minimal performance that an irresponsible person provides?

9. They'll think I've gone nuts.

They might! So what? Madness is so endearing! Just explain.

10. I'll lose my authority.

A manager who manages by coaching gains real respect, as well as self-respect, which is far more gratifying than the illusion of power that props up authoritarians until they fade or fall.

11. I'm an expert and they respect and expect my knowledgeable input.

Your expertise will still be invaluable; only the way in which you will use it will change. Do you begrudge others acquiring some of it from you? Do you dispense your knowledge in small bites, so no one can get enough of it to threaten you? Or do you want to encourage your would-be successors to stand on your shoulders?

12. I already use a coaching style—I don't need to change anything.

One of the classic ways to avoid having to change is to claim that you've already done it. Such people usually have a very poor version of coaching somewhere buried in the bottom of their managerial arsenal. To find out if they use it, ask their subordinates. But be careful, this one may also be one of your own internal barriers. Is it?

INTERNAL BARRIERS

1. It's nothing new—I've done it for years.

If this is your arrogant response, then it's certain that you haven't!

2. I'm afraid I won't do it well.

Without practice you won't. Self-coaching is the least risky place to start. Try it out with the company softball team or with your son or daughter. At work there will be some individuals and teams who are more easy to work with than others. Try it out with them, and tell them what you are doing.

3. I'll get stuck—I won't know what question to ask.

Not if you follow the golden rule of listening to and watching the coachee, and following their interest, lead, or direction. They will always indicate what you should ask. Remember, you are an awareness-raiser, not an instructor. Keep it simple; the whole process is simply variations on the following theme:

What do you want? goal
What is happening? reality
What could you do? options
What will you do? will

4. I won't get the results I get with my old style.

No, you won't. You will soon get *better* results!

5. What I did before worked, why change?

Because your survival and the survival of your organization may be dependent on better performance and better quality of life in the workplace.

6. I don't believe in these new "high touch" approaches.

Too bad, but have you ever tried using one?

7. The only thing that motivates people is money.

Ample recent research shows that that's not true, but it may appear to be until you learn how to offer people something more meaningful.

Now add your list of external barriers to this column, but simply precede each one with the phrase, "*The belief I hold that....*" I do not suggest that your external barriers have no validity out there, but you would do well to acknowledge that a good portion of them are internal ones.

We all prefer to believe that *they* are the problem; it makes us right and saves us from having to change. But it also means we are stuck with the situation because we can't change *them*. If we can admit that it may be our own resistance that we project onto *them,* we are empowered to change things, because they are now under our control!

This is just another instance of how self-awareness and taking responsibility lead to improved managerial performance.

The Multiple Benefits of Coaching 17

*W*hat, then, are the benefits of coaching as opposed to instructing to the manager and the managed, and how does adopting a coaching culture benefit an organization?

This must be the number-one concern, and we would not promote coaching if it did not work. Coaching brings out the best in individuals and in teams, something that instructing does not even aspire to do.

Improved Performance and Productivity

As I stated earlier, developing people does not mean just sending them to a short course or a workshop once or twice a year. The way you manage will either develop them or hold them back. It's up to you.

Staff Development

Improved Learning   Coaching is learning on the fast track, without loss of time from the bench or desk. Enjoyment and retention are also enhanced.

Improved Relationships   The very act of asking someone a question gives them, and their answer, value. If I only tell, there is no exchange. I might as well be talking to a load of bricks. I once asked a particularly silent but promising junior tennis player what he thought was good about his forehand. He smiled and said, "I don't know. Nobody has ever asked me my opinion before." That said it all to me.

Improved Quality of Life in the Workplace   Out of the respect for individuals, the improved relationships, and the success that will accompany this, the atmosphere at work will change for the better.

More Time for the Manager   A staff who is coached, who welcomes responsibility, does not have to be chased or watched, frees the manager to perform his more basic functions. In the past he never found the time to do these functions well.

More Creative Ideas   Coaching and a coaching environment encourages creative suggestions from all members of a team, without the fear of ridicule or premature dismissal. One creative idea often sparks others.

Better Use of People, Skills, and Resources   A manager very often has no idea what hidden resources are available to him until he starts coaching. He will soon uncover many previously undeclared talents in his team. He will also receive solutions to practical problems, which can only be found by those who carry out a task regularly.

Faster and More Effective Emergency Response   In an atmosphere in which people are valued, they are invariably willing to rise to the task when or even before being called on to do so. In many organizations, where people are not valued, they only do what they are told.

The spirit of coaching is all about change, being responsive, and responsible. In the future the demand for flexibility will increase, not decrease. Increased competition in the market, technological innovation, instant global communication, economic uncertainty, and social instability will see to that within our lifetime! Only the flexible and the resilient may survive.

Greater Flexibility and Adaptability to Change

COACHING APPLIED

These are some of the more obvious benefits that accrue for the majority of people and organizations who adopt the regular practice of Performance Coaching. Every business, however, has its unique conditions and requirements and coaching invariably produces both expected and unexpected benefits for organizations. The following are a few examples of how and where coaching is being applied effectively.

> Within the Woolwich Building Society, a growing awareness had developed of the line responsibility for implementing the critical option of management action to support training strategies. The will was present—and much was already happening in various quarters—but this mutual commitment needed a framework to facilitate its universal application.
>
> Coaching was identified as the "missing link" between training input and improved performance. The Grass Roots Group (a company for whom David Whitaker, David Hemery, and I run Performance Coaching programs) was hired to present an in-house program to an audience who was in a position to test the theories and skills across a wide population and evaluate effectiveness using a variety of hard and soft measures.
>
> The power and simplicity of their coaching framework became quickly apparent. Line managers and performers alike responded well to the performer-centered approach, completely in line with a participative management style promoting the underlying

sentiment of "ownership equals commitment." The practice of using effective questions to raise awareness and increase personal responsibility meshed well with existing skills training, particularly across the large Woolwich retail network.

David Stringer, Assistant Training Manager
of the Woolwich Building Society

We have had to become more responsive to public demand while at the same time to use our available resources more efficiently to cope with the increasing workload. The leadership skill of police commanders was strong in the authoritarian role but less effective at using staff in the most productive way. For example, Performance Coaching has been used successfully to encourage officers lower down in the hierarchy to generate innovative ways of increasing our crime detection rate. Recent statistics are very encouraging. Furthermore the GROW sequence of coaching is now used as the standard problem-solving technique at all management levels. Only recently it was used to excellent effect by the chief officers to shape their annual initiatives for the county.

Superintendent Peter Amery, Director, Research
and Planning, Kent Country Constabulary

Coaching is part of the fundamental ethos of our firm. Student accountants have to gain experience on real-life client assignments. This means they have to be coached by their senior who, in turn, will have been coached by their manager or partner. Client satisfaction and working with a budget forces us to coach effectively. In practice, people try to ensure their teams have the best qualified staff, which reduces the coaching load on managers. But cutting corners on coaching overall can be an expensive mistake.

David Thompson, Partner in accountants
KPMG Peat Marwick

We needed to impart coaching skills in a non-manipulative fashion which enabled each individual to develop his own sales management style within an overall framework. Performance Coaching gave us that, but also proved to be a valuable team-building exercise.

Ian Wigston, Director Strategic Planning in Markets Division, Barclays Bank

Garnett Marshall, National Training Director of the British School of Motoring, bluntly and succinctly sums it up for all of us when he says:

Training at BSM is going through a total change of ethos. We think that coaching is a better way of learning than the old-fashioned autocratic way of standing up in front of people. We're aiming for a situation where everyone is coached in a way that encourages them to find things out for themselves. I don't want to be in the business of force-feeding people knowledge. In order to create the right environment for people to learn, the trainer must become a facilitator.

And if all that does not add to more profit, I'll eat my hat.

Coaching to Win

For a final anecdote, let me return to sports, well, at least to a unique and hazardous competitive event. It was renowned for its tradition of authoritarian leadership, which has produced remarkable performances in the past, but which was diametrically opposed to the coaching philosophy.

Every year the highlight of that great military show, the Royal Tournament, held each summer in London, is the Field Gun race. Initiated many years ago to commemorate a heroic campaign in the Boer War in which artillery was transported by men over mountains, the event consists of a race to partially dismantle and drag an ancient gun carriage over an obstacle course daunting enough to most of us without the baggage. The contestants are four branches of the military service.

Each year they are only allowed nine weeks to assemble and train their eighteen-man teams. In 1990, Joe Gough was the first trainer for the Fleet Air Arm team. Before training started, he attended a two-day Performance Coaching course run by my colleague David Hemery and myself. Subsequently, David visited the team in Southampton early in their training. As a result, Joe courageously, radically altered his approach. After the event Joe said, "We changed everything this year, and if we'd failed I'd have been pilloried. However, right now I'm the most popular man in the Fleet Air Arm!"

For the first time in the history of the event, one service won all five major trophies. The Fleet Air Arm "A" team recorded the fastest time, best aggregate time, most points, and fewest penalties. The "B" team also won their trophy. This outstanding result was achieved with 30 percent fewer practice runs than in previous years, and fewer injuries. The team commented:

- "This was the first time that someone had asked our opinion and listened."

- "Joe would ask us if we wanted to do another run, and if we said no, we felt we owed him a bit, and that was a positive carryover to the next day."

- "Joe was very approachable. He treated us like men."

- "One night Joe told us to rig up for another run, and we were shattered. Eric, our PTI [physical training instructor], went and told Joe that he and the team thought his decision was wrong. Joe came out and told us to stow it away! I couldn't believe it. It takes a big man to admit he was wrong…and once he had done that, the rest of us started admitting that we had been wrong on parts of our drill practices, instead of making excuses. There was a lot more honesty all around."

Joe Gough summed up his new-found conviction about the benefits of coaching when he said, "You can *make* a man run, but you can't *make* him run fast!"

For me the benefits of coaching far outweigh the barriers. Do they for you?

Over to You 18

*T*his is a short book about coaching; if it had been any longer you might not have purchased it, or have read this far. I may have included some things that you did not need, I may have left out other things that you might have liked. It may have been too shallow in parts, or too deep in others.

It was my intention to persuade you that coaching is a skill that all people who teach or manage others would do well to acquire. The need for better people skills is growing and will continue to do so in the foreseeable future in business, in the service industries, in our schools, and in sport.

Coaching is not only a tool that managers can use in a wide variety of situations for planning, for problem-solving, for reviewing, for personnel issues, for learning new skills, for personal development, and for team development. It also calls for and generates a more positive attitude toward people, staff, clients, colleagues, customers, and competitors alike.

That adds up to improved performance, faster learning, and a more enjoyable work life for you and those

Grow Your Own

with whom you work. However, your payoff will be closely geared to the commitment you make to becoming a good coach. This book, hopefully, will encourage you to do more of what you already practice if coaching is already your style, or it will set you on a different way of thinking if it is not. It may provide some coaching guidelines within which to begin your practice. It is a map to help you decide where you want to go, but remember, the map is not the territory. That you must explore for yourself, with all its ups and downs, to exhaust and exhilarate you.

I am reminded of a Swiss ski instructor who, after twenty-one years of teaching technique by the "Bend zee knees" school, was ready not only to give up teaching, but to give up skiing too. He was bored by the endless repetition of the same words and exercises with a stream of faceless students. He went to Timothy Gallwey and learned to teach Inner Skiing. From then on teaching took on a new meaning for him, every day was a new challenge, every client became a real person, and his own skiing took him to new heights that he had not imagined possible. Fifteen years later, he is still teaching skiing and loving it. That represents the impact that learning to coach, with its Inner Game origins, has had upon me too. I rediscovered myself, and I discovered the true richness and potential within others for the first time.

Rent a Coach

While acquiring some coaching skill offers benefits to all, there are many circumstances in which bringing in a highly skilled independent coach or facilitator will have several advantages.

Directors of large corporations, and chief executives in particular, may be gregarious, but they can also be very lonely. There are not many to whom they can turn for help, often none in their own organization. Uncertainty about trust and confidentiality, covert in-house competition, and the slipperiness of the corporate ladder often make it hard for a CEO to turn to a boardroom colleague about issues that may concern their peers' performance or tenure. Perhaps even more common, however, is simply the wish to consult a fresh mind, a person who brings no investment or position of his own, an outsider who is not involved with the organization or its culture. An independent coach can reflect ideas, evoke solutions, and support their implementation in a way that few insiders could ever do.

Senior executives are increasingly recognizing the benefits and opportunities for exploring new avenues in consultations with a coach, scheduled on a regular basis. The same is true for senior business teams, who may spend most of their time scattered far and wide. When they do get together, they want their meetings to be as productive as possible, and team facilitation by an independent coach is an excellent way to achieve that. The coach is able to monitor the dynamics of the team and attend to group process while assisting and freeing the team to focus on task. The demand for good independent coaches is growing in all areas.

Do you *grow* your own coaches or hire them as consultants for particular situations? It should be clear by now that all managers need coaching skills, that a coaching culture is likely to engender new heights of performance, and that, even if both of these are in place, there may still be occasions when an outside coach will be beneficial. The answer must be both.

Coaching is a skill. It is not difficult once you have internalized the basic principles. If done well it may become an art, appreciated equally by the coach and coachee. On the next two pages are two simple summaries that can act as a quick guide to the practice of coaching.

The Choice

Here is a repeat of a formula that summarizes the coaching process, but remember it is the *context* we are always striving for, and the *skill* and the *sequence* are simply ways of getting there.

Performance Coaching Is Based Upon:

Context   Awareness and Responsibility

Skill   Effective Questioning

Sequence   G — Goals

R — Reality

O — Options

W — Will

Here is a skeleton set of coaching questions to be elaborated on and used as a guide to a coaching session.

Coaching Questions

Goal	What is the goal of this discussion?
	What do you want to achieve (short- and long-term)?
	Is it an end goal or a performance goal?
	If it is an end goal, what is a performance goal related to it?
	By when do you want to achieve it?
	How is that positive, challenging, attainable, measurable?
Reality	*What (when, where, how much)* is happening now?
	Who is involved?
	What have you done about this so far?
	What results did that produce?
	What is happening both internally and externally?
	What are the major constraints to finding a way forward?
Options	What options do you have?
	What else could you do?
	What if...?
	Would you like another suggestion?
	What are the benefits and costs of each?
Will	What are you going to do?
	When are you going to do it?
	Will this meet your goal?
	What obstacles could you face?
	How will you overcome them?
	Who needs to know?
	What support do you need?
	How will you get that support?
	Rate yourself on a one-to-ten scale on the likelihood of your carrying out this action.

Appendix

Here are some solutions to the nine-dot exercise.

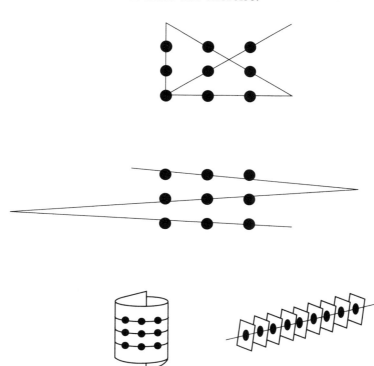

Bibliography

Clutterbuck, David. *Everyone Needs a Mentor: Fostering Talent at Work*. London: Institute of Personnel Management, 1991.

Gallwey, W. Timothy. *The Inner Game of Tennis*. New York: Bantam, 1984.

Gallwey, W. Timothy, and Kriegel, B. *Inner Skiing*. New York: Bantam, 1991.

Gallwey, W. Timothy. *The Inner Game of Golf*. New York: Random House, 1981.

Stayer, R. "How I Learned to Let My Workers Lead." *Harvard Business Review*, November/December 1990.

Kinlaw, Dennis C. *Coaching for Commitment: Managerial Strategies for Obtaining Superior Performance*. San Diego, CA: Pfeiffer & Co., 1993.

Index

A

Accountability, 18-19
  in business, 50
Action
  costs and benefits of, 70
  creating a time frame for, 74
  rating certainty about, 76
  value of, 60
Action plan, constructing, 73-81
Action steps, written record of, 77
Agreement
  on goals, 49-50
  on team goals, 104
Alternatives, exploring, 67-72
Analytical thinking, 31
Answers, attentiveness to, 36-37
Assertion stage of team development, 97-98
Assessment, forms of, 90-92
Assumptions, self-limiting, 68-69
Attention
  to answers, 36-37
  focusing, 30
Attitude
  assessing, 59
  importance of, 23
Authoritarianism, as an obstacle, 111
Authority
  abdication of, 85
  losing, 112
  transference of, 38
Authority models, 13
Autocratic management, 12
Awareness, 22-25. *See also* Self-awareness
  raising of, 30, 89-90
  relationship to skill, 23
  responsibility and, 23

B

Barriers to coaching, 109-114
  external, 110-113
  internal, 113-114
Beamon, Bob, 47
Behavior, modeling of, 103
Belonging needs, 99
Blanchard, Ken, 1
Blind spots, 32
Body awareness, 58
Body efficiency, 35
Body language, 37-38
Body/mind connection, 59
Burness, Cameron, 111
Burnout, causes of, 19
Business
  accountability in, 50
  self-motivation in, 26-27
Business coaching, 7-9
Business success, 84

C

"Carrot and stick" approach, 11
Catchall questions, 76

131

Detachment, 56
Detail, focusing on, 31-32
Discipline, fitness and, 72
Discussion
    democratic, 14
    of team goals, 104
    of team meaning and
    purpose, 106-107
Dynamic tension, in teams, 99

E

Emergency response, effective,
    116
Emotions, tapping, 58-59
Empowerment
    of organizational members,
    86
    of subordinates or coachees,
    39
End goals, 46
Enjoyment, importance of, 87
Environment, safe, 67
Esteem needs, 99, 100
Evaluative terminology, 56-57
Everyone Needs a Mentor
    (Clutterbuck), 9
Example, coaching by,
    103-104
Expectations, going beyond, 83
Experience, working from, 8
Expertise
    changing use of, 112
    of coaches, 34, 35-36
External barriers, 110-114

F

Feedback, uses for, 90
Field Gun race, 119-120
Focus
    on detail, 31-32
    on performance, 87

G

Gallwey, Timothy, 6, 7, 59
Gender, coaching and, 2
Global competition, 17

Goals
    actions leading to, 75
    defining, 43
    imposing, 48
    ownership of, 47-51
    positive stating of, 49-50
    setting, 42, 45-53
    SMART, PURE, and CLEAR,
    48-49
    soundness of, 50
    for teams, 104
Gough, Joe, 120
Grass Roots Group, 117
Greenpeace, 26
Ground rules, for teams, 105
Group dynamics, 98
Group process work, setting
    time for, 105
GROW model, 42-43, 113,
    118, 124

H

Harvey-Jones, John, 14
Hemery, David, 14, 23, 50, 72
Hierarchical relationships,
    power in, 38-39
Hierarchy of needs (Maslow),
    99-100
High-performing teams, 95-96
Honesty, about reality, 63
"How I Learned to Let My
    Workers Lead " (Stayer), 84
How questions, 31, 60

I

Inclusion stage of team
    development, 97
Independent coaches, hiring,
    122-123
Information, sharing, 75
Inner business, 8
Inner conflict, dangers of, 26
Inner courses, 7-8, 34-35, 122
Inner Game, 7
Inner Game of Golf, The
    (Gallwey), 6